D1242080

100 BEST
BARBECUE
RESTAURANTS
IN AMERICA

2016

Johnny Fu

DATE DUE

Cover design by Alessandro Migliorato – Milan, Italy

Cover photos:
Front bottom left – brisket and sausage from Salvage BBQ
Front left middle – pork from Wilber's Barbecue
Front top left – ribs from Bravo Farms Smokehouse
Front top middle – ribs from Hometown Bar-B-Que
Front top left – tray from Freedmen's Bar
Front middle – Johnny at Bates City Bar-B-Que
Back top – Opie's BBQ
Back 2nd – Maurice's Piggie Park
Back 3rd – Gates Bar-B-Q
Back 4th – Skylight Inn BBQ
Back 5th – Central BBQ
Back bottom – Mike Emerson (Pappy's Smokehouse) and Johnny

ISBN: 978-0-9962333-0-9

All photos by Johnny Fugitt except for Chicago q - Lindsey Cavanaugh, Eat Pray Photo;
The Shaved Duck - courtesy of The Shaved Duck

Some names and identifying characteristics have been changed.

Every effort has been made to make this book as helpful and accurate as possible. As the
restaurant world changes every day, the information for restaurants may have changed
since publication.

The 100 Best Barbecue Restaurants in America

Caution: Side effects of this book may include late night cravings, spontaneous road trips and the meat sweats. Not all material may be appropriate for vegetarians. Carnivore discretion is advised.

Introduction

Barbecue is American art. It's the smell and taste of our great country. Despite unresolved debates over our national cuisine, we find beauty in the diversity of our backgrounds, tastes and traditions. Barbecue is the quintessential American meal for a gathering of friends, families and communities. Barbecue reaches all demographics and walks of life. It's meant to be shared. The smell of barbecue transports us to another place and time, yet defines comfort food for the here and now. It's historic and traditional, yet current and evolving. The smell of smoke is common throughout the world, but we created our own unique methods, tastes and styles to produce something distinctly our own. Distinctly American.

Barbecue means summertime and baseball. It means road trips and returning to one's roots. It means urban hole-in-the-walls and small town joints where everyone is known by name. It means third-generation families working long hours to uphold the family name as well as entrepreneurs chasing a dream. It means more to restaurant owners than making a living. It means providing for their children, creating jobs for their neighbors, giving to their communities and creating something that makes people happy.

Early in Julia Child's career, she was spurned by editor after editor who said Americans were unwilling to give the time and effort necessary to follow Julia's French recipes. These editors were, as you know, wrong. The pace of life has only increased since Julia's time, but the popularity of barbecue, a food that requires even more time and effort than French cooking, has increased as well. This paradox actually makes sense. The busier we become, the more we appreciate that which takes significant time and effort to create.

Food is about more than sustenance. Good food slows us and reminds us to enjoy life. No food requires as much time and effort as barbecue and no food provides the same sense of place, people and purpose. It's part of who we are as individuals. It's part of who we are as a people.

In one year, I did two things that speak to the American spirit. First, I hit the open road. My barbecue travels took me to the 48 contiguous states. I met owners, pitmasters, chefs, managers, servers and bartenders who make American culture, as well as America's barbecue. Second, I did something unprecedented. No one had attempted a project like this. I visited more barbecue restaurants across a greater geographic area in a condensed amount of time than anyone. Ever!

This book is the summation of that experience. It started with the question "What are the best barbecue restaurants in America?" and ended with a story as well as an answer.

The Beginning

Our culture is obsessed with lists and rankings. *Buzzfeed* successfully digitized the crack cocaine that is cultural rankings and now every smartphone in America deals this addictive substance 24 hours a day. At a superficial level, there is something in us that wants to visit or experience "the best." At a deeper level, though, experiencing anything at its highest level, from architecture to a pork sandwich, is experiencing beauty and art.

When a local writer or reporter publishes a ranking of the best burgers, drinks or things to do in town, I'm all over it. In the last five years, nearly every city has received a list like "Top 5 Barbecue Restaurants in New York", "Best of Birmingham's Barbecue" or "The Top Ten BBQ Joints in Austin." For most of these lists, a writer will visit 10, 20 or 30 local barbecue restaurants to pick their favorites. Their opinions are, of course, subjective, but they back up their rankings by explaining their preferences, tastes and reasoning.

When you look at the "10 Best Barbecue Restaurants in America" lists, and there is a new one every week on click-sucking sites like *Eater, Thrillist, Huffington Post*, etc., you find lists that should instead be titled "The 10 Most Historic Barbecue Restaurants in America" or "The 10 Best Marketed Restaurants in America." Some of these lists do not provide authors. When one list cited an author, the writer was forced to eat smoked crow when he admitted to not visiting all of the restaurants on the list - let alone visiting others to determine that those on the list were really the best. Some lists are nothing but marketing in the same vein as the "Best Steakhouses in America" ads you see in airline magazines. Other lists are conglomerations from multiple writers. A national publication might ask a handful of writers from places like Kansas City, Texas, Memphis, the Carolinas, D.C., New York, Chicago and California for nominations and push them all together.

These methods, obviously, have their flaws. I wanted to see the local model used at a national scale and was surprised no one had done it. Barbecue books are big business these days, but they primarily focus on history, recipes or technique. Since I could not find an extensive, well-researched guide to barbecue restaurants, I saddled up the Subaru and hit the road. As you will soon see, it was the adventure of a lifetime.

As soon as I shared my project to anyone while traveling, I was peppered with a number of questions. How did you decide which restaurants to visit? Did you eat the same thing at each restaurant? What kind of barbecue do you prefer? First, I want to share my methodology and answer some of these burning questions you may have. Second, in just one chapter, I'm going to share much of what I learned about barbecue over the course of the year. I'll share a few stories from the road and proceed to my list of *The 100 Best Barbecue Restaurants in America*. At the end, I have an awards section (Top 10 Ribs, Top 5 Baked Beans, etc.) and a quick reference guide.

Crisscrossing America: Project FAQ's

Why barbecue?

Everyone thinks themselves an expert on three things: God, Politics and Barbecue. These three topics elicit firmly entrenched views, debate and disagreement. I have always been a casual barbecue enthusiast and wanted to fan the flames of the great barbecue debate. I spent some of my childhood in Kansas City and North Carolina and remember visiting Kansas City favorites like LC's as a teenager. My amateur attempts with the backyard smoker only increased my appreciation of barbecue restaurants.

Who are you to make this list?

I'm not a competition barbecue participant or judge. I'm not a restaurateur. I'm not a trained chef. I am, however, the person who has visited more barbecue restaurants across a greater geographic area in a condensed amount of time than anyone. Daniel Vaughn, *Texas Monthly*'s Barbecue Editor, has visited more restaurants than me, but over many more years and without the same geographic spread. One of the best barbecue books on the market is *Peace, Love and Barbecue* by Mike Mills and his daughter Amy Mills-Tunnicliffe. The book is primarily a cookbook, but they also profile a number of historic barbecue restaurants. Their research took them to 15 states and Mike has eaten more barbecue than just about anyone in America, but I still covered more ground at beltbreaking speed. I gave barbecue restaurants in non-barbecue country the opportunity to be compared to the Black's and Arthur Bryant's of the barbecue world. I gave smaller, newer, rural or less-acclaimed restaurants *in* barbecue country the opportunity to compete against the big boys who receive all the press, accolades and attention.

My professional work in the kitchen is limited to a season with a Sicilian Chef in London. I lived with a pair of Polish girls and six Italian guys while in graduate school. The Italians were in England, purportedly, to learn English as they worked. Their behavior suggested, however, that drinking and carousing were their primary objectives. My housemate, Michele, worked in the kitchen of a Sicilian restaurant, and, a few days before Valentine's Day, called to ask if I was interested in washing dishes for the busy Thursday-night holiday. I agreed. At the end of the night, Chef Paulo asked if I would work Friday and Saturday since the restaurant would be busy all weekend. This turned into every weekend.

After a while at the dish station, the Americano, yours truly, was allowed to help make pizzas, ensaladas and antipasti, but never allowed out of the kitchen, lest any patrons see me. When cocaine-fuelled Chef Paulo graced the dining room with his presence, Michele and I took pulls from the bottle of cooking wine. If Chef Paolo ever noticed the bottle being a little lighter after checking on the dining room for a couple minutes, he never let it be known.

Chef Paolo made plates of seafood risotto or pasta for Michele and me each evening, which we inhaled as we tried to get out of the kitchen as quickly as possible. There was one meal each week, however, when the staff gathered like a family, took our time to eat and actually sat down. On Sunday afternoons, Chef Paulo prepared traditional Sicilian fare not found on the menu and two or three nicer bottles of wine would be passed around. One such Sunday, Chef Paulo's English friend (and cocaine dealer) joined us. The bloke went on and on about how great his recent trip had been to Napa and Sonoma. "The only problem," he said "was there were too many bloody Yankees." The table turned to me as if the insult was more injurious than the ribbing I took from them on a daily basis. I just kept eating.

How did you decide what restaurants to visit?

I'll use Memphis as an example to answer this question. I had to visit Rendezvous which is one of the most famous and historic barbecue restaurants in America. Rendezvous may have been the driving force behind transforming ribs from a throwaway cut of meat into a barbecue staple and American favorite. Central Barbecue was another must-visit as it is often considered the favorite of Memphians and cited as one of America's best.

Memphis Barbecue Co. is run by a pair of celebrated barbecue competition winners including the most decorated female competitor of all time, Melissa Cookston. The Germantown Commissary was mentioned as one of the best in town by a number of barbecue restaurant owners outside Memphis. It has also received plenty of press and is spoken of as one of the best in the country. Payne's is a hole-in-the-wall in a rougher section of town whose followers are as ardent as any. The biggest local chain, Corky's, serves more barbecue in Memphis than anyone. B.B. King's combines barbecue and blues on Beale Street. Pig on

Beale and Blues City Café also serve racks of ribs on Beale with one being older and the other a relative newcomer. Pop's Smokehouse is a food truck that came recommended by a barbecue guy I met on my way to Memphis. Tom's Barbecue is an old-school spot that was featured on *Diners, Drive-Ins and Dives*. Double J's is one of the newer kids on the block in downtown Memphis. Showboat and Three Little Pigs are older, but less heralded joints. One and Only is a newer place that has received some positive local press.

There are other barbecue restaurants in Memphis with a lot of history, loyal followings and national reputations. Jim Neeley's is one of these places. I was unimpressed with my visit a few years ago, so it wasn't a must-visit place for me despite its well-known name. Instead, I gave that spot to a smaller, hole-in-the-wall in hopes of discovering a hidden gem. Had I not done that, I might not have discovered one of my favorite places in Memphis.

I visited restaurants big and small. White tablecloth restaurants and hole-in-the-wall joints. Established as well as newly opened. Nicer parts of town and rougher parts of town. Old-school style and new-school approaches.

I didn't want to compile a list of the most famous or historic places in America, but I had to visit these for my project to be complete. This list included Joe's Kansas City (formerly Oklahoma Joe's), Arthur Bryant's, and Gates in Kansas City; Rendezvous and Central in Memphis; Skylight Inn, The Pit and Maurice's in the Carolinas; Dinosaur as the best known in the Northeast; Moonlite Inn in Owensboro, Kentucky; Big Bob Gibson's in Alabama; Franklin in Austin and the big three in Lockhart (Smitty's, Kreuz and Black's).

Some of these historic and famous restaurants are still excellent places to go for a meal. Some of the big names, however, live off their reputation and no longer produce great barbecue. McClard's

Bar-B-Q in Hot Springs, Arkansas, was one of those places. McClard's is Arkansas' most famous and historic barbecue restaurant, but I was disappointed to see a plate of ribs warmed in the microwave before being sent out of the kitchen. I'm pretty sure that's not how things were done when they opened in 1928 and it's not how things should be done today.

Apart from this group of restaurants who have national reputations, there are plenty of others who are known throughout their neighborhoods, cities or regions as some of the best. I tried to hit many of the most respected restaurants, but my sample could only skim the surface of the vast pool of barbecue. I heard 10,000 thrown around when I inquired to the number of barbecue restaurants in the country, but I haven't been able to verify this number. Almost all of these restaurants, even the ones most people consider to be quite poor, have customers who consider them the best. I could never hit everyone's favorites, but I still have the biggest sample to date.

I generally stayed away from the big chains like Famous Dave's. I did, however, visit Dickey's in Logan, Utah, when I found myself in an area of over 100,000 people with no local barbecue options. Obviously I prefer local, family-run places with character, but, in Dickey's defense, I've had much worse barbecue than I found at Dickey's. They did not make the Top 100, but a massive fast food chain from Texas can still put out better barbecue than many local restaurants in the northeast and western half of the country. I have, by the way, a list of areas with a shortage of barbecue restaurants for any aspiring barbecue entrepreneurs. If you like to ski, the Logan area might not be a bad place to open shop.

The four main centers of barbecue were, as you might expect, where I visited the most restaurants. I made 43 stops in Texas, 35 in Missouri, 27 in the Carolinas and 24 in Tennessee. There were a few states where I visited more restaurants than you might have expected (22 in California and 11 in Pennsylvania, for example) and a couple where I did not visit quite as many as I would have liked (5 in both Mississippi and Kentucky). There were a handful of states, like Idaho, where I made a single token stop. Although I made more visits in Texas than any other state, if I were doing this again, I would make an even greater percentage of my stops in Texas. There were some notable places like La Barbecue and Snow's that I did not get to visit. From what I hear, these may have been some of my favorites.

Did you try the same thing at every restaurant?

No. I generally tried whatever each restaurant considered to be their signature items. This obviously varied region to region, but it also varied restaurant to restaurant within a given city. "What do you consider your signature items?" was a standard question during my visits. Sometimes I would receive a straight answer and other times I would hear something like "Picking my favorite dish is like picking my favorite child – I just can't do it", "Everything is my favorite. I wouldn't serve it otherwise" or "Throw a dart. It's all good."

When I had meetings set up with owners, pitmasters or managers, I would often receive a sampler plate. When I didn't have a meeting set up, I would look online for tips, ask the staff for recommendations or try a sampler plate. If I had multiple restaurant visits scheduled for a day or did not have high expectations for a restaurant, I ordered something small, like a sandwich and one side. If that impressed, I would order something else. If not, move on.

While I focused on the staples of barbecue, I enjoyed sampling the unusual items I came across on my journey. From snoot to congealed pig skin, barbecue beignets to barbecue fish 'n chips, I tried it all.

Did restaurants want to meet with you?

For the most part, yes. Restaurant owners know the power of external recognition and praise. A positive review in the local paper draws more business than thousands of dollars of advertising in the same paper. Owners often thanked me for writing this book, visiting their restaurant and giving them a shot. One owner told me they were on the brink of bankruptcy eight years prior before Guy Fieri of *Diners, Drive-Ins and Dives* stopped in. The publicity provided the boost in business to stay open all these years. I do not have the reach of the *Food Network*, but every little bit of exposure helps. In addition to local media requests, most restaurants have frequent catering tastings so my visit was nothing unusual.

Most of the big barbecue restaurant names in the country (like Rendezvous, the Lockhart big three, Skylight Inn, Big Bob Gibson's, Joe's Kansas City, Central, etc.) were very welcoming. A couple of the biggest names in barbecue, like Franklin Barbecue, did not respond to my interview requests. I get it. When Anthony Bourdain and Daniel Vaughn consider you the best in America, what was to be gained by meeting with me? I'm sure Aaron Franklin has a constant flood of media requests and he is also busy doing things outside of the restaurant like filming a TV show. I like to think this didn't affect my rankings. Franklin is, after all, a Top 10 place. While I loved talking shop, seeing the smokers and having a drink with the owners, I had to leave off many of the nicest people I met along the way because I didn't think the barbecue was quite at the same level.

For the most part, the restaurants without national reputations were eager to meet with me. A few places, more old-school, mom-and-pop restaurants in small towns were a bit wary and would ask questions like "Are you trying to sell me something?", but the vast majority of people seemed genuinely excited to share their story, show off their barbecue and hear about my project.

Approximately two-thirds of my visits were planned in advance where I had meetings set up. As I mentioned, a few did not respond to my interview requests, but were still places I wanted to visit. Others were unplanned stops. In San Francisco I took a flyer on a restaurant a friend's coworker's cab driver said was the best in town. It was in a rougher part of the city and none of the other restaurant owners had even heard of it. I really wanted it to be fantastic and to help discover a hidden gem, but it was forgettable at best. I asked gas station attendants and anyone I could find for recommendations. I sought the most local guidance outside barbecue country where my research turned up limited options, but responses in these parts tended to range from "Everyone loves Famous Dave's" to "You mean…like…burgers and stuff?"

What was a typical restaurant visit like?

My planned meetings lasted anywhere from half an hour to four hours. It depended on how talkative the restaurant owners/managers/pitmasters/chefs/staff were. I started most conversations by inquiring as to what made their restaurant and food unique. I then heard stories of how they got into barbecue, learned about the food, asked about local or regional barbecue perspectives, toured the kitchens, inspected the smokers and sat down for a plate of food.

It was a concern that I may have eaten differently than the regular customer by scheduling an interview. I learned so much about the restaurants through these interviews and tours, though, I accepted the trade-off.

Did you eat barbecue every day?

No. I averaged one new restaurant visit a day for a year, but did not eat at a new restaurant every single day. I actually preferred to eat at multiple restaurants one day and then take a few days off. This helped me avoid barbecue burnout. The most visits I completed in one day was eight in the Atlanta area. I did not feel great that night and do not recommend this. Eight restaurants in one day was the result of a tight travel schedule.

While I did not eat barbecue every single day, I actually ate it more than 365 times. There were a couple of restaurants I visited twice and I couldn't say no to friends and family when they wanted me to try their backyard barbecue to see how it compared. I'm in the Navy Reserves and my shipmates wouldn't let me get away with not trying the ribs at the galley, Ney Hall, in Newport, Rhode Island, while we were there for training.

What did you look for in a restaurant?

I looked for places with character and mmmm-inducing, belly-rubbing, eye-rolling good food. I wanted to visit a variety of restaurants, but I always looked for character. Strip malls are never good, but it wasn't a kiss of death as a few restaurants on the list overcame this. I like places that make their food from scratch. Most restaurants claim to prepare everything from scratch, but my questions and tours often revealed information to the contrary. A surprisingly high number of restaurants use commercially produced barbecue sauces as bases and "doctor them up." Roughly one tenth of the restaurants I visited serve okra, but probably 90% of these serve frozen okra. Fresh okra has a limited season, but how could made-from-scratch describe dumping something from a bag into a fryer? Some restaurants serve potato salad or slaw straight out of a tub from Sam's Club. Others use microwaves to reheat, hold meat overnight or freeze and reheat. While I care more about what I am served than how they got it there, these are generally not the best practices. By setting up meetings, I gleaned these bits of information I would not have picked up by dining undercover.

I started with a rubric that guided my thinking throughout the process. Some barbecue people argue that barbecue is about nothing but meat. Meat is certainly the most important factor in any barbecue meal. Most people consider more than meat in their restaurant experience, though, so I did the same. Out of 100 points, my rubric was set up like this: Meat (40 points), Sides (20 points), Sauces (20 points), Atmosphere (10 points), Barbecue "It" Factor (10 points).

Meat: I did not favor any particular meats, but, for example, compared one restaurant's pork ribs to hundreds of other pork ribs around the country. I prefer meat served either dry (no sauce) or minimally sauced. The best of the best need no sauce as the meat is just too good to mess with. If barbecue is pre-sauced, it becomes a sauce competition. The meat should be able to stand on its own and if meat is drowned in sauce, it's most likely because it's not very good. The customer should be able to add sauce as desired. Have I covered all of my sauce cliché bases?

Sides: I ate more baked beans, potato salad, slaw, greens, mac 'n cheese and cornbread in the last year than in my previous 29 years combined. I also found a number of unique sides or twists on traditional recipes along the way. Finding something fresh, made-from-scratch and with a little bit of character was important to me.

Sauces: As mentioned, great meat needs no sauce. With a killer sauce, though, I'll mop it up with a piece of white bread or fries and shovel it in. Like meats, I tried not to let my style preferences create inordinate bias, but, for example, compared each mustard sauce to other mustard sauces and the sweet, tomato-based sauces to other sweet, tomato-based sauces.

Atmosphere: Generally what I looked for is character. A strip mall setting with wagon-wheel décor is uninteresting, overdone and expected. A white tablecloth restaurant with modern art could score well as could a trailer on the side of the road with a few picnic tables. A restaurant just needs to have an identity, be interesting and be unique.

Barbecue "It" Factor: Restaurants scored low if they took shortcuts with their food. The scored low if they played Top 40 music (country, blues, rock, folk…polka…anything but Top 40 in a barbecue restaurant is acceptable). They scored well if they sourced quality local ingredients and the owner splits wood from his family's farm. They scored well if it's a place you want to stay after you finish your meal. They scored well if there is a view other than the parking lots of Best Buy, Marshall's and Taco Bell.

Does service factor into this?

Service played a minor role in the Barbecue "It" Factor. I didn't look to be pampered at a barbecue restaurant and there is a wide range of behavior I consider acceptable. A smile and "sir" never hurt, but I also don't mind being quickly pushed aside by a busy cashier. A couple things do turn me off. Spare me the corporate speak. "Welcome to Pit-Smoked Bill's. I'm Pit-Smoked Suzy. Can I start you off with a Pit-Smoked order of fried pickles? How about a Sugary Southern Sweet Tea? It's a Pit-Smoked Bill's special!" Disinterested high school kids who did not care if they worked at a barbecue restaurant or Wendy's annoyed me, while staff who had been with the restaurant for 20 years was a plus.

When I asked one waitress in New Mexico what she recommended, she said the brisket was "fall off the bone tender." I couldn't help but laugh in her face. In other places, staff would say, with deepest sincerity, "our ribs are smoked for three hours" believing this to be impressive. One West Coast owner kept going on and on about Kansas-style barbecue (which his was not). I'm not sure if he thought Kansas City was in Kansas or if he wanted to pay homage to the barbecue of Wichita, Topeka and Manhattan. One larger, less-enthusiastic waitress in Tennessee, in an apparent effort to minimize steps, hinged at the kitchen door as she rotated between yelling at her customers and the kitchen staff. I didn't mind being yelled at. It was the yelling back that was unnerving.

Don't your personal tastes play a big factor in this?

Sure, food is subjective. Tastes are subjective. More on this later.

What style of barbecue do you like?

I often heard it said that the best kind of barbecue is the barbecue you grow up with. There is some truth to that, but my regional preferences evolved as you will see in the upcoming chapter.

Is there a restaurant on the list from every state you visited?

No. While barbecue from places like Maine, South Dakota and Washington did make the Top 100, I failed to find barbecue in Arizona and New Hampshire that would pass as average in barbecue country. In total, restaurants from 28 states and Washington, D.C., made the list.

How did you keep track of all of these restaurants?

I visited a lot of restaurants, ate a lot of the same foods and covered a lot of ground. Some of it ran together, but I filled seven sticky notebooks with restaurant details and took thousands of pictures to help keep things straight. Blogging about most of the restaurants at www.barbecuerankings.com also helped.

Where did you find the worst barbecue?

It was my goal to highlight the best in barbecue, not dwell on the worst or drag anyone's name through the mud. On more than a handful of occasions I blogged about bad barbecue, but, more often than not, highlighted the best part of an underwhelming experience. There is some really bad barbecue out there and I found some of it. You can find bad barbecue anywhere, but it is much more common the further you travel from the South.

My three stops in Delaware were frighteningly bad. I had nightmares about Delaware barbecue for months. If you measure the worst state for barbecue by number of local barbecue options, though, North Dakota might be at the bottom. North Dakota has Dickey's and Famous Dave's, but I was only able to find two local barbecue options in the whole state. Although barbecue was a major part of the menu at these two restaurants, they also served steaks, pastas, pizzas, burgers, etc., so they were not strictly barbecue restaurants. One was not good, but Spitfire Bar and Grill in Fargo was pretty good. Give me Spitfire any day over barbecue in Delaware, but let's at least give Delaware credit for having local, barbecue-only restaurants.

One restaurant in Colorado told me they use liquid smoke on their brisket – the cardinal sin of barbecue – and served pork so poorly cooked it could not be pulled, but was, instead, sliced like a ham. This had to be one of the worst visits of the trip. One tip for finding poor to mediocre barbecue is to look near the gates of a military base. I think they survive because military personnel rotate so frequently the restaurants do not have to earn repeat business. A disproportionate amount of the military also comes from the South and Texas, which can't hurt. I recommend you steer clear.

How are you so skinny/how much weight did you gain?

If I had a rack of ribs for every time I heard "Never trust a skinny food writer" or "I thought you would be fatter" or "You don't look like you have eaten at hundreds of barbecue restaurants" I think the ribs would stretch from coast to coast.

Let me introduce you to The Barbecue Rankings Diet – all the barbecue you can eat and still lose weight. I weighed 147 pounds at the start of this project and weighed 145 pounds when I finished. I have always been thin and a year of barbecue didn't change anything – arteries possibly excepted. I attribute my barbecue weight loss to five factors.

First, when I wasn't eating barbecue, my diet was healthier than ever before. I ate more salads. Instead of cookies and chips for snacks in the car, I traveled with delicious fare like prunes, nuts, bananas, chia seeds and flax seeds. I ate a lot of banana pudding, pecan pie, bread pudding, carrot cake and ice cream at barbecue restaurants, but tried to limit my sugar intake otherwise.

Second, I juiced most of the way. My Jack LaLanne power juicer traveled with me, but I eventually juiced it to death with about two months left in the project.

Third, I jogged when the weather, schedule and motivation permitted. I must maintain physical fitness standards for the Navy Reserves which was also a nice incentive.

Fourth, I have the skinny genes to help fit into skinny jeans. I have my father to thank for that as we are about the same size.

Fifth, I tried to limit my eating at each restaurant. Sampling a few items at each restaurant was still a lot of food, but I rarely cleaned my plate. I wasted a lot of food, but often took leftovers to friends or in search of someone hungry on the street.

I am not the only skinny person in barbecue. A number of restaurant owners told me they actually lost weight after opening their restaurants. Being on your feet for 14 hours a day is a good way to lose weight. Most, however, still take their work home with them each night. A skinny barbecue owner in Arkansas told me a story about a pair of larger, African-American ladies who walked into his restaurant, found out he was the owner and left after commenting how they didn't trust a skinny white boy to make barbecue. Skinny man barbecue discrimination is real.

What has this done to my health?

I did not think to have my cholesterol checked before I started this project, so I can't do a *Super Size Me*-esque before and after. While I didn't put on weight, gastrointestinal emergencies were not rare.

Whichever diet program you subscribe to, my diet didn't fit it. I ate a lot of meat, but if Paleo is your thing, I ate way too many carbs, dairy products and sweets. I consumed a lot of fat, a lot of salt, plenty of blackened or charred meats often accused of being carcinogenic and a surprising amount of sugar. I had plenty of carbs from sandwiches and cornbread while most of the greens were prepared in some sort of grease.

After the project, I created Recovery Month. A dietician put together a salad-heavy meal plan for me. I exercised daily and refrained from alcohol and sweets (well…for the most part). I didn't go vegetarian, but I ate a lot less meat. I worked my way through the entire menu at Chop't, a New York and D.C. area salad chain. Had I made salads at home, I wouldn't have lasted more than a week, but the variety at Chop't kept me going. I'm no dietician, but my thinking is that barbecue isn't bad for you. Like anything, though, it should be consumed in moderation.

Are you tired of barbecue?

When I finished my travels, I certainly needed to take a break from barbecue. It didn't take long for me to get right back into it, though.

Some restaurants commented that they wished I had visited early in the Barbecue Rankings Tour before I was tired of barbecue. People at the beginning of the project, though, commented that they wished I had visited at the end of my trip so I wouldn't forget about them.

While I have a newfound appreciation for top notch barbecue, I have less patience for average barbecue.

How much did this cost?

A small fortune. People joked I undertook this project to get a bunch of free barbecue, but, one look at my bank account will tell you that this was not free barbecue. A flight from D.C. to Seattle, bus ride to Portland, and flight home, for example, made those five plates of barbecue pretty pricy – even if a couple of them were free. I bought hundreds of plates of barbecue, drove over 31,000 miles, paid for flights, had all the normal costs of life and was unable to do much other work for a year and a half. I could make the case this was the most expensive barbecue anyone ever had.

I did however, have a few generous sponsors. Ole Hickory Pits signed on near the beginning. Thanks also go to Big Town Tickets; Widespread Properties; Nashville, Springfield (MO) and Northwest Arkansas franchises of Happy Feet and the aforementioned Chop't.

Did you get a lot of free barbecue or swag?

Yes, most of the time when I had a meeting set up I would get free food, but I always offered to pay when I didn't think my host would be insulted. Most of the time I would get a response like "No way!" or a dismissive "Oh, please". Other times, an owner would practically talk through the menu as if everything was a signature item. "You have to try our ribs and the pork is fantastic. People rave about our mac 'n cheese. Our jalapeno poppers are the best I've ever had and I'm a jalapeno popper fanatic. Our carrot cake won best in Smith County two years ago and its grandma's secret recipe. Oh yeah…you HAVE to try the chicken wings." I went with their recommendations and found myself with a bunch of food I didn't want and a $60 check. It all averaged out.

T-Shirts, sauces and rubs were the most common swag, but pint glasses, bags, hats, coozies, etc. all made it into the swag bag. Some people gave me stuff knowing it would be a giveaway item on my blog – a cheap marketing expense for them. Others noticed that I wore barbecue shirts to restaurants, thus providing a bit of advertising to people who eat and make barbecue. I think I genuinely made some friends along the way and they wanted me to have a memento of my visit. Some, I'm sure, simply hoped a hat or shirt would make my review a touch better. Although one restaurant joked about giving me money, no one did...or tried. I would probably have made a lot more money by listing restaurants with friendly marketing professionals and multiple, professionally operated restaurants with gift shops by the door, but it wasn't worth it. Just as many restaurant owners work hard to keep the integrity of the restaurant since their name is on the front door, my name will always be on the front cover of this book.

What was the hardest part?

Hundreds of people commented that I was living their dream, and I certainly was on the adventure of a lifetime, but there were some challenging aspects to the project. The most difficult was that I wanted to include so many more restaurants on my list. After hearing about the struggles of owning a restaurant, how hard most of the owners work, what the restaurants mean to their communities and feeling like I made new friends, it was hard not to include them in the list. This list, however, isn't the 100 nicest people I met along the way. Only 100 of my 365 visits (27%) made the list. The last thing I want to do is put a subpar plate of barbecue on the list for you to try.

Most barbecue restaurant owners genuinely believe they belong in this book. Behavioral economist Dan Ariely discusses a phenomenon in his book *The Upside of Irrationality* I noticed in barbecue restaurants. Ariely called it the "IKEA effect" after putting together a piece of furniture from IKEA and feeling particularly proud of his work. If we create something, we view it irrationally. We are not objective in our valuation of our own creations; hence, I'm already preparing my James Beard Award acceptance speech. Many owners told me they don't like to eat at anyone else's restaurant because they like their own barbecue better. Some of this is differences in taste, but I bet a lot of it is the "IKEA effect." I'm sure some owners will be surprised not to be in the Top 100.

Did you drive or fly?

Both. I drove over 31,000 miles this year – far enough to drive all the way around the equator *AND* take a trip from New York to Los Angeles *AND* drive from Seattle to Miami. How's that for a road trip? I had to drive most of the way since many of the barbecue restaurants I wanted to visit were in small towns, but I also flew to eight cities.

Were you traveling all the time for a year?

No. I am in the Navy Reserves which required me to be in St. Louis or D.C. about once a month for my weekend drill. I took three or four week looping trips between drills most of the time.

You must not be married or have kids, right?

Correct. For all of its joys, I may have barbecue to blame for my dating drought - that and rarely staying in the same state for more than a week at a time. A 2006 study separated a group of men into a heavy red meat eating group and a non-red meat eating group. After two weeks, women smelled auxiliary pads with the men's scents and the groups were then flipped – the meat eaters abstained and the non-red meat eaters binged on steaks and burgers.

The results were clear...and sad. "...repeated measures analysis of variance showed that the odor of donors when on the nonmeat diet was judged as significantly more attractive, more pleasant and less intense. This suggests that red meat consumption has a negative impact on perceived body odor hedonicity."

If there was any biological significance to eating red meat, I would have thought women to be attracted to the men eating a lot of red meat – presumably the best at acquiring the red meat. Perhaps cavemen with the red meat didn't share. I don't know. With as much red meat as I ate, I was a walking Glade dispenser of red meat pheromones. Unfortunately, my experience verifies the clinical trials that a red-meat heavy diet doesn't attract the ladies.

BBQ101: A Barbecue Primer

I considered myself a casual barbecue fan before beginning this project, but I admit to not knowing much about the kinds of smokers used by restaurants, the different cuts of meat or the deeper nuances of regional styles. Toward the end of my trip, a friend who joined me for a restaurant visit said he didn't understand much of my conversation with the restaurant owner as we discussed some of the details of his preparation and service. Through hundreds of conversations with restaurant owners, I learned a lot about barbecue. When I had the idea for this book, I surveyed the vast pool of barbecue literature to make sure nothing quite like this existed, but did not read much of it. Almost everything in this chapter I learned from restaurant owners, pitmasters and managers across the country.

I'm going to share stories, observations and a few best practices in this section. There are some nearly universal best practices, but nearly every rule is broken by someone making great barbecue. I would hear one restaurant owner say that you must burn green wood, trim the fat a certain way and allow meat to rest before serving. Two hours later, an owner across town would insist upon using seasoned wood, not trimming the fat and serving it as promptly as possible. Both restaurants might make great barbecue and both believe their methods to be superior.

A number of food shows and documentaries have visited the Tokyo fish markets at the break of day. It's a bustling madhouse filled with the city's top Chefs trying to find the freshest, most pristine fish. Anthony Bourdain interviewed famed New York and Tokyo sushi master Naomichi Yasuda who, despite being one of the best in the world, stays completely out of this fray. Instead, he strolls through the market late in the day, picks out lesser cuts of fish and freezes these cuts for about a week. He doesn't care that his practices are outside the norm. He does it his own way. Sometimes excellence breaks the rules.

Regional Styles

Before beginning this project, I was able to identify the big four regional styles of barbecue. I associated the Carolinas with vinegary pulled pork. I knew Kansas City was famous for burnt ends and tomato-based barbecue sauces. I knew Memphis was all about ribs while Texas was brisket country. I knew each of these regions claimed to be the center of the barbecue world, but had no idea how strongly these beliefs were held until visiting each of them. Every few years, *Texas Monthly* puts out the most comprehensive barbecue restaurant list in the Lone Star State with its Top 50. On the cover of the 2013 edition was the title "The 50 Best BBQ Restaurants ~~in Texas~~ in the World!" People in Texas joked that half of my work finding the 100 best barbecue restaurants in America was completed by *Texas Monthly*.

Whether in Kansas City, Texas, the Carolinas or Memphis, I would often hear comments such as "well, you know we are the capital of barbecue", "obviously your number one spot has to be from here" or "barbecue isn't barbecue unless you _____"(do something their way). People in the Carolinas, for example, think it an assault against their way of life to call brisket barbecue. They have been making it the longest, so they should have some say in this conversation.

In 2009, Anthony Bourdain wrote an article titled "13 Places to Eat Before You Die" with Oklahoma Joe's (now called Joe's Kansas City) on the list. Bourdain reasoned that "It's the best BBQ in Kansas City, which makes it the best BBQ in the world." Praise like this bolsters the ego of any Kansas Citian, and every region likes to recycle this kind of accolade.

While everyone has their favorite region, it's fair to say each of these regions has the history, moan-inducing barbecue and published superlatives to claim to be the best. There is some truth to the claim that the best barbecue is the barbecue you grow up with, but I also uncovered any number of unsubstantiated claims of superiority. Memphians aren't the only ones to say this, but I've heard them say the worst barbecue in Memphis is better than the best barbecue from anywhere else. A conversation in Memphis might go like this:

Me: Do you think Memphis has the best barbecue in America?

Memphian: Well of course we do! We have the history, tradition and the best restaurants in America right here.

Me: What restaurants have you tried in Kansas City or Austin?

Memphian: Well, I haven't been to any of those, but brisket ain't barbecue. Kansas City is too far north to serve real barbecue.

Me: Well, what about the Carolinas? They were doing it long before Memphis, right?

Memphian: I don't know about that, but if they were, we took what they started and perfected it. Listen, anyone in Memphis will tell you we have the best barbecue. Everyone here knows it and people from all over the world come here for the barbecue. It's just a fact.

This reminds me of another observation from behavioral economist Dan Ariely. He uses a story from Mark Twain to illustrate the "Not-Invented-Here" bias which says that "If I (or we) didn't invent it, then it's not worth much." You and I may be quick to dismiss this view as petty, but Twain's impenitent disdain toward his countrymen's choice of stoves may help shed some light into the matter. Twain observed that the German wood burning stoves were much more effective, efficient and economical than the American stoves of his day. Americans could have adopted the better stove design, but, "According to Twain, Americans turned up their noses at German stoves simply because they hadn't come up with the better design themselves."

This "Not-Invented-Here" bias makes sense when we think about barbecue. I consistently heard that a different meat, style of sauce or way of smoking isn't barbecue and I think the "Not-Invented-Here" bias helps explain this. When you combine the "IKEA effect" of being overly proud of something you make with your own hands, and the "Not-Invented-Here" bias towards the style of your own region, we find restaurant owners firmly entrenched in the belief that their barbecue is the best.

The big four make up the top tier of barbecue regions because they made unique and important contributions to the barbecue world. Carolina kicked things off with whole hogs, vinegar sauce and the pulled or chopped pork sandwich. Texas brought us the brisket and German immigrants in the Lone Star State made sausage part of barbecue culture. Memphis' claim is, of course, ribs while Kansas City's contribution includes burnt ends and tomato-based sauces. The four most common components in barbecue today are pulled pork, ribs, brisket and tomato-based barbecue sauce – one item from each of the four main barbecue regions.

Before moving on, I should point out that Carolina barbecue typically refers to North Carolina and this can further be divided into two distinct categories of Eastern Carolina and Western Carolina. Eastern Carolina is traditionally chopped whole hog with a clear vinegar sauce while Western Carolina is predominantly pork butt or shoulder with a vinegar-based sauce that includes a little tomato or ketchup. Likewise, Texas has its own regional styles. Barbecue means very different things to people in Houston, Lockhart, West Texas, the Hill Country and along the Mexican border.

In the background of all the grandiose boasting of the four main regions, plenty of other places like to stake their claim in barbecue. I separated these into two more regional tiers based on their contributions to barbecue. The second and third tiers might not get the national attention of the big four, but visit any of these locations and their sense of place in barbecue history is almost as strong.

I put three places into this second regional tier of barbecue.

South Carolina: South Carolina is known for its distinctive yellow or golden mustard sauce. These vinegar-heavy sauces work great with pork and when a mustard sauce is done right, it's hard to find anything better.

North Alabama: North Alabama's contribution to barbecue is the iconic white sauce. Imagine a mayonnaise-based ranch dressing thinned with vinegar and heavily spiced with black pepper. It's best used on chicken.

Western Kentucky: Owensboro, Kentucky, claims to be the capital of barbecue and their unique contributions to the barbecue world include mutton and a thin dipping sauce not all that dissimilar from au jus.

I have four areas on my third tier of barbecue regions.

St. Louis: St. Louis is a city most people associate with barbecue thanks to St. Louis-style ribs. St. Louis-style ribs, though, are not a particular style as much as they are a cut. More about this soon.

Georgia: In some ways Georgia lacks a barbecue identity as it mostly pulls from the Carolinas or Alabama, but their contribution of Brunswick stew puts it on the third tier of barbecue regions in my mind. The improving barbecue restaurant scene is finally starting to reach a level of respectability worthy of the unofficial capitol of the South.

Nashville: Nashville will always be the step-brother to Memphis when it comes to barbecue in Tennessee. Besides, Nashville has enough good things going for it so let's at least let Memphis have barbecue. Nashville makes this third tier thanks to their contribution of the cornbread pancake. Often used instead of a bun, it makes the perfect complement to a pork sandwich and I hope it spreads throughout the barbecue world. Like St. Louis and Georgia, the barbecue restaurant scene here is improving.

California: The land of the tri-tip. Despite making a meat contribution to barbecue, the fact that tri-tip doesn't have the geographic reach and, frankly, isn't as good as ribs, pork or brisket, keeps California in the third tier of regions. Most people not in the Western time zone are altogether unfamiliar with it. Tri-tip is a smaller, tough cut of beef from the bottom sirloin. It is the centerpiece of Santa Maria-style barbecue which is, to be nice, mostly ignored by anyone outside California.

This tiered approach to barbecue regions does not mean restaurants in these regions fall within these tiers. I think a number of restaurants in "third tier" places like St. Louis and Nashville stack up well with their "first tier" neighbors of Kansas City and Memphis. St. Louis and Nashville simply haven't given as much to the barbecue community as Kansas City and Memphis.

You might notice I failed to include one geographic area that has received a lot of attention lately: New York City. For every person reading this and shouting an exuberant, Texas-twanged "NEW YORK CITY!?!" there is another who has seen all of the press proclaiming New York as either *THE* center or *A* center of American barbecue. I absolutely loved one place in Brooklyn, but found the scene as a whole overhyped. The barbecue scene in New York has grown and improved in the last 15 years, as it has almost everywhere, but New York has the microphone to make us all hear about it. Besides, New York shouldn't be in this tiered section because they haven't contributed a cut, sauce or style to the barbecue world.

Choosing which region is the best in barbecue isn't all hyperbole. In addition to blind enthusiasm for the home team, each locality can make logical cases to their claims. The top five states for barbecue restaurants per capita are 1. Oklahoma, 2. Georgia, 3. Alabama, 4. Missouri and 5. South Carolina. Interestingly, Tennessee, Texas and North Carolina are outside the Top 5 (North Carolina is 17th). In percentage of restaurants that serve barbecue, we see some of the same states. When measured by percentage of restaurants that serve barbecue, Alabama takes the prize with a whopping 8.27%. Arkansas is second. Georgia is third. Tennessee and Mississippi are 4th and 5th respectively. You could make the case, statistically, that Alabama deserves to be considered the best in barbecue.

Much of this regional chest thumping boils down to different perspectives. There is plenty of hometown bias, but you can also look at objective evidence. Take the question "Who are the five greatest musicians of all time?" If you ask 20 people, you will likely get 20 different answers. Someone could argue Michael Jackson, Pink Floyd, Whitney Houston, the Eagles and AC/DC since *Thriller*, *The Dark Side of the Moon*, *The Bodyguard*, *Their Greatest Hits* and *Back in Black* were the best selling albums ever. The Beatles, Elvis, Michael Jackson, Madonna and Elton John, however, have sold more total music when you add all of their albums. One could look to the past and point to Mozart, Bach, Beethoven, Brahms and Wagner. Someone might put a list together like Johnny Cash, Louis Armstrong, Elvis, Mozart and Jay-Z by listing, arguably, the five biggest names in five different genres. Another person might take the same approach, consider the exact same genres and come up with George Strait, Duke Ellington, The Beatles, Bach and TuPac. Another would go the same direction but use different genres and pick Bob Marley, Stevie Wonder, Scott Joplin, Led Zeppelin and Frank Sinatra. Some would turn to artistic contribution more than sales or public notoriety which would lead to discussion of Roy Orbison, Miles Davis, Bob Dylan, Eric Clapton, B.B. King, Radiohead, Jimi Hendrix, David Bowie, and John Coltrane among others.

Which answer is correct? There isn't exactly a right answer or a wrong answer. It's all about perspective. Barbecue is similar. Personal tastes and opinions play into it, but objective measurements should also be part of the conversation.

What styles or regions do I enjoy most? I started as a Kansas City guy. It's what I grew up with. After learning about the different styles and eating my way across America, my regional preferences changed.

The best city for barbecue today is Austin, Texas. As you can tell by my rankings, there is a lot of great barbecue to be found all across the country, but Austin is my favorite for five reasons. First, the brisket in Texas – and in particular Austin – is at a whole different level from brisket anywhere else. In most regions and restaurants, the pork and ribs will be much better than the brisket, but when brisket is done right, it's my favorite bite in barbecue. Second, in addition to brisket, Austin does everything else well. A great town for foodies, Austin has adopted and recreated the ribs, pork and sides from other regions. Believe it or not, some of the best pork and ribs can be found in Texas. Third, Lockhart is only a short drive away. Eating isn't only about the food. It's partially about the experience. I love places with character and history. Austin joints have their own character, but they lack the history of other regions. Luckily, some of the most authentic, old-school barbecue experiences you will find anywhere in America are located a short drive away in Lockhart. Fourth, I appreciate Texas' devotion to serving meat dry (without sauce). Texans believe that if meat is prepared the way it's supposed to be prepared, you shouldn't want sauce. Before starting this project, I was a guy who would cover meat in sauce, but once you try the best of the best, you won't go back. As the clichés go, the meat should be able to stand on its own and if it's covered in sauce they probably have something to hide. Finally, out of my 365 barbecue restaurant visits, my favorite was in Austin.

No city may be more proud of their barbecue than Kansas City and they have much to be proud of. The perfect burnt end is one of the best bites in barbecue and sauces like Gates keep me coming back for more. I still have a special place in my heart for Kansas City barbecue.

While it's surprisingly difficult to find barbecue on the most iconic streets in Austin (6th Street) or Kansas City (Country Club Plaza), Beale Street in Memphis follows the pattern of blues bar, barbecue joint, kitschy tourist souvenir shop repeated over and over. Barbecue is a greater part of the identity of Memphis than any other city in America. People in Kansas City, Texas and the Carolinas argue about which barbecue restaurant is best while

Memphians argue about whose backyard produces the best barbecue.

Finally, I have to say I was a little bit disappointed in the Carolinas. The ironic thing is that I default to pulled pork and either a vinegar-heavy North Carolina sauce or mustard-based South Carolina sauce. I also love the history and ambiance of many of the restaurants in the Carolinas. I would rather take the terrific sauces of the Carolinas, however, and add them to the meats from elsewhere. I never came to love the chopped-to-oblivion pork on a plain bun. I loved the sauces and while nine restaurants from the Carolinas (six North, three South) made the Top 100, including one in the Top 10, I never quite got it.

I also came to deeply enjoy some of the local specialties from the second and third tier regions such as Brunswick stew and the cornbread pancakes from Nashville. Some restaurants like to incorporate local flavors and preferences into their barbecue. One restaurant in D.C. adds Old Bay to their rub as a nod to the crabcake and seafood loving nearby Marylanders. Sides like fried plantain can be found in Caribbean-influenced areas of Florida while salads are much more common in health-conscious California. Green Jello is a thing in Utah, so Holy Smoke BBQ in Layton serves a small cup with each plate. I was told the origins of this have to do with the ease and affordability of Jello with many church and family gatherings occurring in the heavily Mormon state. Finally, when requesting water at a San Francisco barbecue restaurant, I was asked "Still or sparkling?" I was more likely to be asked "Tap or hose?" at most barbecue restaurants.

When asked to name their style of barbecue, owners outside barbecue country most often responded in one of three ways. First, they gave a definitive, one word answer of "Texas", "Memphis", "Carolina" or "Kansas City." This group of owners tried to be as true as possible to a particular style. Their goal was to replicate and honor a particular tradition. A second group claimed to pull from a few different regions. "Our brisket is Texas-style, our pork is Carolina-style, our ribs are Memphis-style and our sauces are Kansas City-style. We try to take what is best from each region and pull them all together." Sometimes it worked, most of the time it didn't. A third group responded by saying, "We learned things from other regions, but we really have our own style." This leaves room for innovation without having to reinvent the wheel. These restaurants are not trying to live up to anyone else's standards, but set their own.

Smokers

From holes in the ground to brick pits, submarine-like tanks to commercially produced rotisserie smokers, I knew there were a variety of smokers when I began this project. I did not know, however, how passionate and committed people are to their chosen style or brand of smokers.

The most popular way of smoking meats at barbecue restaurants today is with large, commercial, rotisserie-style smokers. These range in size from dishwasher to college dorm room. The four main brands are Ole Hickory Pits, Southern Pride, J&R and Cookshack. Full disclosure, Ole Hickory Pits was a sponsor of the Barbecue Rankings Tour, and while Southern Pride has a large following in the South and J&R has a following in Texas, Ole Hickory Pits is the industry leader. I often decry the major publication's Top 10 lists as basically being "The 10 Most Historic Barbecue Restaurants in America", but will point out that on the Forbes list, for example, 5 of the Top 10 restaurants use Ole Hickory Pits.

These rotisserie-style commercial smokers have a number of benefits. One of the keys to creating great barbecue is maintaining a consistent, steady temperature. This style of smoker achieves consistent temperatures better than any other by being well insulated and automatically lighting more wood if the temperature starts to dip. Some of my favorite baked beans are smoked in this style smoker as the drippings from the meats fall into pans of beans on lower racks. These smokers also allow a restaurant to load it with wood, leave it overnight and know that their meats will smoke at precisely the preferred temperature. The main criticism of these smokers is that they use gas flames to start the wood and lose a little bit of authenticity that way. While these machines are easy to operate, they still require a practiced eye and experienced touch to know when the meats are finished.

The iconic Texas pit looks like a septic tank. No other smoker produces a brisket like the best of these smokers. They do, however, have their drawbacks. First, they use a ton of wood so they are more expensive to operate. Second, you lose consistency with these smokers. They require a deft, experienced hand to operate which means if the pitmaster leaves or is gone for the day, the barbecue may or may not be the same. I talked to an owner in Texas who wanted to open a second location, but was unable to do so because he understood the barbecue wouldn't be the same with someone else operating a different pit. The seasoning, lineage and aging of this style smoker is important as I often heard "The taste is in the walls" and restaurant owners will boast from whom their smokers came.

There are also historic places in Texas that use brick pits. Some of these use indirect heat and slow smoke while others are closer to grilling with direct heat.

The traditional brick pits are what you see in some of the old Memphis restaurants and across much of the South. These range in size and style, but many have tall brick walls on three sides, a rack about five feet off of the floor with either smoldering coals or a live fire underneath. The secret of these pits, one owner told me, is that the droplets of grease fall from the meats directly onto the coals which sizzle, create a greasy steam and provide moisture in the pit.

While every region and barbecue person has their own position on smokers, Texans have the deepest held beliefs and are happy to tell you about it. Daniel Vaughn, the most trusted writer on Texas barbecue, is not a fan of the commercial rotisserie smokers. Multiple restaurant owners in Texas believed they were not given a fair shot to be listed on the *Texas Monthly* list because they use rotisserie-style smokers.

This stance against commercial rotisserie smokers reminds me of the Amish. Technology was allowed to develop for centuries, but should be abjured past a chosen point in time. People have smoked and cooked meat over flames in some sort of hole in the ground, primitive oven or pit for thousands of years. Smoking in a manufactured, rounded steel tank (often placed on a trailer) was a huge technological jump and is a relatively new practice. The tank defenders argue barbecue should be done the "traditional way" with their style smoker, but their steel tube isn't traditional either. It's only the traditional way of smoking if your view of history is quite short.

I think watches provide a useful analogy. Imagine an old guy saying he will never wear a digital watch because he believes a timepiece should include a face and hands. At first this seems traditional. To a Swiss watchmaker, though, the Made in China, battery-operated face watch is more similar to a Made in China, battery-operated digital watch than the hand-crafted, mechanical watches his family has made for hundreds of years. Having a watch with a face does not necessarily make it "traditional."

Similarly, tank purists should recognize that they are not preparing barbecue the oldest way possible and accept that if they embraced technology up to a certain point with the advancements of using plated, formed steel on trailers, they shouldn't be so quick to criticize the use of more advanced technology. If anyone has the right to bemoan the use of modern technology in barbecue, it's the old-school folks in the Carolinas. Smoking meats mostly the same way for multiple centuries, they should be the only ones to judge a guy with a 20th century smoker (tank on a trailer) or a 21st century smoker (the rotisserie).

Keith Allen of Allen & Son Bar-B-Q is someone who has earned that right. He does everything in an old-school manner which includes hauling his own wood and splitting it behind the restaurant. He works long hours, but does things just as he did 44 years ago when he opened the doors for business with $452 in his pocket after investing $6,000 in the restaurant. He believes in his methods, but when asked if he considered himself a purist or traditionalist, he told me, "No, I'm just crazy." There are a lot of easier ways to make a living, he said, and some in barbecue are just looking to run a business and make money. I appreciate his hard work and dedication to his craft.

My final point on this topic is that even Daniel Vaughn's best of the best, Franklin Barbecue (who I also put in my Top 10 and think is phenomenal), wraps their briskets in butcher paper and holds them in what is essentially an electric warming oven. I don't mind this because Franklin produces an incredible product, but it seems hypocritical to criticize the use of a rotisserie smoker while accepting the use of an electric oven as a method of holding meat. Going back to my Amish analogy, it's kind of like the Amish riding in a car, but refusing to drive. It just doesn't make sense to me.

If I strike up a conversation with someone in Texas and they want to judge my credibility as a voice on barbecue, they'll ask for my position on smokers just as they would ask a politician for his/her stance on an important social issue. If I do not line up with them philosophically on this vital issue, I may hear mutters about the waywardness of my generation or that they shouldn't let foreigners (from Missouri) into Texas.

I've had great barbecue from all varieties of smokers and pits. I've had average barbecue from all varieties of smokers and pits. I've had bad barbecue from all varieties of smokers and pits. I care more about what is plated than how they got it there. I admire hearing stories about a restaurant being in the same family for generations or an owner chopping all of his own wood on the family farm, but if the plate doesn't measure up, it doesn't matter.

There are certainly better ways of operating. I prefer locally sourced, hormone-free and antibiotic-free meats. Can I tell this by a bite? Probably not. Fresh, hormone and anti-biotic free meats are generally of a better quality, but this is certainly not the deciding factor in how good the barbecue will be. I prefer my sauces not to have High Fructose Corn Syrup. Can I taste it? Sometimes I can guess it's there, but not always. All of this is to say it matters how you get the food onto the plate, but how you get smoke into meat isn't nearly as important.

It is important, however, that there is smoke. It isn't barbecue if there isn't smoke. I had, for example, a great plate of *food* from The White Swan in North Carolina. The White Swan has been serving barbecue in rural North Carolina since the 1940's. I emphasize that I had a great plate of food, rather than barbecue, at The White Swan for two reasons. First, my favorite items were the Brunswick stew and fried chicken – food associated with barbecue, but not necessarily smoked. Both were incredible and the Brunswick stew is one of the best you will find anywhere. I wasn't all that impressed with the rest of the meal, but thought having a couple top notch peripheral items might be enough to get them on the list with passable pork and a good sauce. Unfortunately, when they decided to franchise in 2009, Federal inspectors shut down their process of smoking with oak. Instead, they have to cook with electric in order to ship to each franchise location. (Most chains have smokers at each location, but the transportation of cooked food is apparently what tripped up The White Swan.) I have no problem saying that The White Swan gave me a good plate of food, but I can't say that they gave me a good plate of barbecue since smoke wasn't in the equation. Electric smokers are not ideal, but at least they burn wood chips, chunks or sticks. Using essentially an oven, however, just doesn't cut it.

A common theme from restaurant owners is that increased regulations are making their work more and more difficult. Employee and compensation laws often present challenges to staffing. Sanitation laws have forced many of the old-school restaurants to continue to change practices through the years. In some locales, inspection fees that were once nominal or non-existent have been raised, shifted to the restaurants, and viewed as revenue producers by the city since restaurants are forced to pay hundreds of dollars for an inspection. One restaurant uses a pellet-style smoker because their city requires stacks of wood to be sprayed with pesticide every month. "Mmm…is that a hint of organochlorine insecticide I'm picking up on the pork?"

The most common local regulations, though, are regulations placed on smokers. Many large cities, most often on the West Coast or in the Northeast, have enacted laws against smokers for environmental reasons. To some, the banning or strict regulation of smokers is for air quality reasons. A ban against smokers is also a way for animal rights activists to target restaurants that serve meat.

These bans are not limited to blue states, though. There is only one barbecue restaurant in Houston cooking with a traditional Texas pit. Pizzitola's was grandfathered into the current regulation, but the law still hangs heavy over the operation of the restaurant. They are unable to make any significant changes to the restaurant – build a patio, expand the dining room, etc. – or they would lose their grandfathered status. New restaurants are forced to use a commercial smoker or leave the city limits. In other cities, a variety of smokers are allowed, but the equipment needed for the ventilation, filtering, etc. is cost prohibitive to opening a restaurant.

Even in small towns, I talked to owners who said the city made them change how they smoked their meats due to complaints from neighbors. Barbecue often thrives in rural areas, but these can also be the strictest when it comes to alcohol sales and this can make a big difference to the bottom line of a restaurant.

One of the great things about barbecue is that it transcends socio-economic lines. You are likely to see luxury cars and clunkers in the same barbecue restaurant parking lot. Not that long ago, a man could put a smoker, case of meat and cooler of beer in a parking lot and, essentially, create a business. The barriers to opening a restaurant today are often too great for this to be a viable option to someone without means, but with the willingness to work. Excessive regulations hurt barbecue. Excessive regulations hurt the American dream.

Wood

A conversation about smoke naturally leads to a conversation about wood. Wood use varies region to region, but hickory and oak are most commonly used. Varieties of hickory and oak also vary region to region. Woods like apple, cherry, peach or pecan are common, but often more expensive depending on local availability. Other restaurants use ash, mesquite or walnut.

The old-school Texas restaurants in Lockhart have cord after cord of post oak sitting outside to age for a year before smoking. Different restaurants have different philosophies on this. Some insist upon seasoned wood while others prefer greener woods. Some restaurants prefer to keep the bark on the wood while others prefer to have it removed. Some season their woods in different ways such as dunking the wood in a water and apple juice bath right before smoking. One restaurant only uses whole rounds from the trunk.

Some restaurants are quite protective of their wood secrets and will not share their supplier or even hint to the area from which their wood comes. Some restaurants ship their wood thousands of miles across the country to get exactly what they want. Others will burn anything they can get their hands on. One restaurant in Arkansas burns scraps from a nearby hammer handle factory.

Some restaurants essentially offer a free tree removal service to source their wood. One restaurant has a relationship with an orchard where they provide pruning services and keep whatever they want for the restaurant.

Some restaurants mix varieties of wood while others separate the woods based on the meat they are smoking. Some will start on oak or hickory and finish with a fruit wood believing this to add a hint of sweetness at the end.

In addition to the kind of wood used, there are dozens of different ways of using the wood. Some restaurants only allow the wood to come near the meat when it has burned down to coals. Many have preferred ways of stacking the wood as it burns. Some restaurants haven't let the fire in their smoker die out for decades and even tend the fire on Christmas morning – they take this very seriously. I go to such lengths to share some of these methods to make the point that there are literally hundreds of ways of using wood in barbecue and wood is just one factor in the final product.

Rubs

Rubs are spice mixtures applied to the meats (normally before smoking, but sometimes during or after as well). Some restaurants let the meats marinate in the rub overnight or for a few hours before smoking while others apply a rub immediately before it hits the smoker. Exceptions exist, but pork rubs are sweeter while brisket rubs are spicy or savory. The basic pork rub includes heavy doses of brown sugar and paprika with lesser amounts of salt, pepper, mustard and cayenne. The recipe then goes a thousand different directions.

For briskets, many of the absolute best in Texas use nothing but a 50/50 mix of salt and pepper. Garlic, paprika and cayenne are often mixed in. Brown sugar is occasionally used, but it's not common. Brisket rubs go fewer directions than pork rubs, but I tried beef rubs with coffee grounds, cocoa, Hispanic-influenced spices and Jamaican jerk inspiration.

Restaurant owners tend to go one of two directions with their rubs: extremely secretive or bare-it-all-to-the-world open. Let's start with the latter. The 50/50 salt and pepper brisket guys in Texas are not only open about their simple rub, but preach it as brisket gospel. Others are happy to share their rubs because they do not see it as the key to great barbecue. Great barbecue is produced, in their minds, by proper smoking techniques. Sharing their basic rub recipe is almost a way of bragging about how they can produce great barbecue with something so simple.

On the other end of the spectrum, I often heard things like "The pork rub contains brown sugar, paprika, salt, pepper, cayenne, mustard powder and a few more special ingredients I can't tell you." Mike Mills, one of the most successful and respected men in barbecue, famously did not share all the ingredients of his quintessential Magic Dust with his competition team, but had each of his teammates add a few spices when the others were absent. Some owners were happy to share all of the ingredients in their rubs – including things like coriander, cinnamon and onion powder – but said the secret was finding the right balance of spices.

Whether meat is served wet or dry (with or without sauce), most restaurants use a dry rub. Some who add sauce during or after smoking do not use a dry rub while others do not use any rub or sauce but let the meat go au natural. For briskets, I like a simple salt and pepper rub. For pork, I like an element of sweetness, but still prefer savory and spicy notes to be featured.

Sauce

As I mentioned earlier, I started out as a guy who would lather as much sauce onto a sandwich, forkful of meat or French fry as possible and considered it barbecue. This is one style of barbecue, but it is no longer my favorite. I now prefer meat served naked or dry. I do not mind restaurants putting a dash of a vinegar-heavy sauce on pulled pork, but it should compliment more than cover. I consider this dash of vinegar seasoning rather than saucing. Similarly, I do not mind ribs that are basted with a mop or sauce during smoking, but sauces should be added during the smoking process so the moisture largely evaporates and the ribs are sticky rather than runny (but not too early where the sugars burn). Right next to liquid smoke, saucing an excellent brisket is a cardinal sin. 99% of the brisket outside Texas, however, is better with sauce because it isn't really brisket. Instead, it's sliced, cooked beef from the brisket cut.

All my conditions aside, an excellent sauce is a great compliment to meat – in particular to America's most popular barbecue meal, the pulled pork sandwich. Pulled pork should be served naked or with minimal sauce so the customer can taste the meat and add the amount and style of sauce he or she chooses. Some restaurants only have one or two sauces, but most carry four to six. A few restaurants have sauce bars with up to 100 different sauces, some of which are produced in-house and others brought in for customers to sample. Over the course of the Barbecue Rankings Tour, I sampled over 2,000 sauces. While most are similar, there is a huge spectrum of flavors and styles.

America's most popular sauces are sweet and tomato-based, but I started out with a preference for more spicy, tomato-based sauces. Not habanero hot like a hot sauce, but black pepper spiced tomato sauces like Gates'. After the journey, my favorites are North Carolina vinegar-heavy, blended with a little bit of tomato sauces and rich, vinegary South Carolina mustard sauces.

The range of sauces is rapidly expanding and copycats are prevalent. I tried coffee or espresso sauces in no less than ten restaurants. Fruit-based sauces (raspberry, blueberry, etc.) are everywhere. Sauces with hints of alcohol flavoring are popular. Some restaurants age their sauce for a few days while others serve it fresh. Even after 363 restaurants, I discovered something new with an orange flavored sauce at my second to last restaurant visit. Most restaurants serve sauces at room temperature, but I appreciate warmed sauces. White sauces (with mayonnaise and/or eggs) are normally the only ones that need to be refrigerated.

Most restaurants, and of course the best ones, make their own sauces. Some restaurants have grown to the point where they must produce off-site in a commercial packaging company, but as long as they stay true to their recipe, I don't mind this.

Meats

Barbecue is (almost) all about the meat. Without quality meats a barbecue restaurant should permanently close the doors, but the best restaurants also feature quality sides and sauces to create the ultimate barbecue experience.

Great barbecue starts with quality ingredients. As one owner told me, "You can't make chicken salad out of chicken shit." Unfortunately, the quality of meats restaurants use is all across the board. Sourcing is important. The best restaurants work with local farms and have a great relationship with a local butcher or butcher in-house. Many of the best insist their meat is never frozen and inspect every piece before it hits the smokers. Others use boxed cuts of varying qualities from national suppliers. One restaurant in Ohio purchases beef raised by the Ohio penitentiary system. You can start with a great product and make terrible barbecue or make quality barbecue from lesser cuts of meat, but, generally speaking, if you start with a better product, you will end with a better product.

An owner of a smaller, less successful restaurant told me about his travails to source from the same local farm as the larger, nationally known restaurant across town. After asking the popular restaurant's staff where they source their pork and not receiving an answer, he resorted to dumpster diving behind the restaurant to find boxes with some sort of markings or address. He proudly now serves the exact same cuts of meat (but not as successfully or tastefully I should add).

Consistent butchering and sizing is key to having a consistent end product. Ribs, chicken, briskets, pork shoulders, turkeys, etc. all vary in size and this is a challenge for restaurants. I was surprised to see many restaurants cooling and reheating meat. Although I think the food loses a little during this process, I found some restaurants able to put out a great product this way. Most restaurants claim to smoke fresh every day and any unused meat goes in the beans, another side or is tossed. I had my suspicions about this, though. Other restaurants made no bones about smoking, chilling and serving a few days later.

A basic understanding of the differences in ribs is helpful to the casual barbecue fan. The four most common cuts of ribs are baby backs, spare, St. Louis-style, and rib tips. Baby backs are the smaller ribs with the higher arch from near the backbone of the hog. These tend to be leaner and were a less desirable cut until an advertising campaign made them popular with a catchy jingle. Spare ribs are the bigger boned, meatier and fattier ribs around the pig's side. A spare rib consists of the main rib bone with a fattier end that can include smaller bones and cartilage. When this section, or tip, is cut off, you have rib tips as well as St. Louis-style ribs (the long bone section).

A few restaurants serve deep-fried ribs or flash-fried ribs. Some barbecue folks turn up their noses at these as either destruction of good ribs or the masking of bad ribs, but they can be quite tasty. Most often they are the unsold ribs from the day before, but I still enjoy one occasionally.

People colloquially use pork shoulder and pork butt interchangeably, but they are different. Both are from the shoulder of a pig and the term "butt" refers to the end of the shoulder closest to the body. When separated, the end opposite the butt is called the picnic. Some restaurants use butts and some prefer whole shoulders. One owner deemed the bone of a shoulder a "flavor rod." Smoking with bone-in shoulders seems like it would impart the most flavor, but I can't say, after having hundreds of each, that one is necessarily better than the other.

I came to loathe what I call "Sloppy Joe barbecue." It can be found with brisket, but pork is most often the victim. Sloppy Joe barbecue isn't just sauced meat, but meat that is sauced and languishes in a pan covered in its own grease. The quality of the meat when it entered the pan might not have been terrible, but, by the time the corpse is found, things have gotten unquestionably ugly.

Brisket has a lean end and moist (a.k.a. fatty) end. I liked to sample both, but, when given the choice, went with the fatty. A poorly executed brisket is cooked meat with needless fat. On a quality brisket, the fat will not be overpowering and, instead, turn a good bite into a great bite. If you are new to Texas barbecue and try some of the highly rated places in this book, be sure to try the fatty end of the brisket. Brisket is the meat that oxidizes, changes and dries out the fastest. If you order a sampler plate, always begin your meal with the brisket. Most barbecue folks say a brisket is the most difficult meat to serve at the highest level. I agree. Anyone can make edible pulled pork. It's not easy to make quality ribs, but they can be found in a lot of places. There may only be a couple dozen places in America, though, making elite brisket.

Texans refer to brisket, pork ribs and sausage as the Texas trinity. I prefer to define the Texas trinity as brisket, sausage and more brisket. This doesn't mean great ribs are not to be found in Texas. It means Texas is all about the brisket. I kept sausage in the mix because no other region does sausage like Texas.

As the sayings go, sausage making isn't pretty. Most barbecue restaurants outside Texas buy commercial sausages. Some are from big distributors while others work with local butchers or regional packers. It's much more common for restaurants in Texas to make their own and the best of the best go the extra mile. Sausages are sometimes all pork, sometimes all beef or sometimes a blend of the two. Occasionally something like turkey or chicken will be thrown into the mix as well. I tend to prefer spicy sausages, but always like trying the unusual blends. One of the

Top 10 Sausages came from McGonigle's Market in Kansas City who does things a bit differently. Rather than fill a casing (some restaurants use natural casings while others use artificial casings), McGonigle's adds extra binding agents and smokes the sausage as a loaf. These pork loin sized sausages are served by the slice.

Beef ribs have a tornado-chaser-like following. Most people stay away from beef ribs. If they want ribs, they go for pork. If they want beef they go with brisket. People who love beef ribs, however, are fanatical about them and hunt them. I stress the thrill of the chase because beef ribs are not easily found. First, most barbecue restaurants do not serve them. Many people outside the Texas to Kansas City corridor, which I call Beef Alley, will have never seen them. Second, the restaurants that serve beef ribs often do not put them on the menu or take them off when prices rise too high. A meat-eorologist's forecast for beef ribs puts a salivating chaser in the car, ready to go.

Chicken recently overtook beef as America's most consumed meat. Often grilled, its place in barbecue is tenuous because grilling isn't barbecue (grilling is high, direct heat vs. the low, indirect heat of barbecue). The casual interchange of the two terms is infuriating to many in barbecue, myself included. Many barbecue restaurants do not serve chicken, but, those that do, typically serve halved chickens, pulled chicken, wings or fried chicken. I found a few excellent smoked half chickens, but most were uninspiring. The chicken dishes that made my Top 10, though, will make you reconsider your go-to pork or beef.

Pulled chicken can be good, but I found it often to lack flavor. I love great chicken wings and there are a variety of styles to be found at barbecue restaurants. Some serve smoked wings while others smoke first and then flash-fry or deep-fry. Some are dry-rubbed, others are covered in more traditional barbecue sauces and a few reach outside traditional barbecue flavors.

Fried chicken is inseparable from barbecue in North Carolina. I found some great fried chicken there, but no one in barbecue does it better than Lillie's Q in Chicago. I haven't eaten as much fried chicken as I have barbecue, but it's right there with Gus's in Memphis as the best fried chicken I've ever had.

Turkey is becoming more and more popular in barbecue restaurants across the country. I was never inclined to try the turkey when pork or beef were on the menu, but it's grown on me. It's a healthier option that restaurants say appeals to women, makes for an excellent vehicle to showcase a great barbecue sauce, and, to be honest, beats anything you can do at home. When it's done right, a smoked turkey beats grandma's Thanksgiving turkey.

Burnt ends are a Kansas City specialty and one of my favorite bites in barbecue. Burnt ends come from the fatty, point end of the brisket and thus require extra time in the smoker. Smoking methods for burnt ends vary, but the point is separated, smoked further and cubed. The results are heavily rubbed and charred bites of meat candy.

Some restaurants feature these meats in dishes like tacos, burritos, nachos, or stews. One dish becoming more and more popular is a layering of ingredients (often beans, slaw, potato salad, meat and sauce) in a single dish called a Redneck Sundae or BBQ Sundae. Some restaurants use ice cream sundae glass dishes and stick a pickle spear in the top to imitate the straw. I wouldn't want to see my favorite barbecue turned into something like this, but it is a tasty treat for a barbecue lover. Other regional specialties include mutton in Kentucky, Tennessee Round Steak (bologna) along the Memphis to St. Louis corridor, pork steaks in St. Louis, and ham, most often found in Kansas City. I found barbecue fish 'n chips at one restaurant in Pennsylvania, but it does not come with my endorsement.

Sides

Like a distinctive drink or appealing atmosphere, superb sides enhance a barbecue experience. The most common barbecue sides, found in all corners of the country, are beans, slaw and potato salad. Beans range in style, but sweet, baked beans with chunks of pork, beef or sausage are most common. Many restaurants place unsold meat from one day in the baked beans for the next. In Texas and the Southwest, pinto beans with hints of Mexican flavors are quite common.

Slaw can be both a source of pride and a point of contention. While Memphis and the Carolinas insist slaw top a pulled pork sandwich, many outsiders despise the practice. Slaws are generally divided into two camps. The most common slaw is the creamy, mayonnaise-based slaw. I find it bland. The vinegar-based slaw most commonly found in the Carolinas, on the other hand, packs a punch and pairs well with pork. Whether using jalapeno, horseradish, garlic, bleu cheese or some other flavor, I appreciate something unexpected in a slaw to make it interesting and distinctive. I believe it best for a restaurant to feature a couple of unique sides. Many people will not appreciate something like a vinegar-heavy slaw with cilantro, lime and a touch of cumin, but this side will help build restaurant identity, create a following of its own and make the experience memorable.

I found potato salad varieties to vary less by region and more by restaurant. Again, some of my favorites had more character than a typical potato salad. A chilled, baked potato salad with sour cream, bacon and chives was appreciated as was a warm potato salad with cubed potatoes topped with a light vinegar and tarragon dressing.

Other popular barbecue sides include mac 'n cheese, greens, Brunswick stew, corn, okra, fries, sweet potatoes, barbecue spaghetti, hash 'n rice, cornbread, hushpuppies and pickles. It's easy to produce a bland, inexpensive pan of mac 'n cheese (remember church potlucks?), but a quality mac 'n cheese is indicative of a restaurant that takes their sides seriously. Greens were never my favorite, but I found a few I thoroughly enjoyed. Many are made with meat drippings, but I think the two keys to quality greens are getting just the right amount of vinegar and maintaining texture and crunch by not allowing them to cook to a soggy pulp.

Brunswick stew is a specialty of the Eastern Seaboard from Virginia to Georgia. I rarely found it far from this area unless the restaurant had a connection to this portion of the South. While some might say a stew doesn't seem like it fits with barbecue, Brunswick stew is a combination of many ingredients we associate with barbecue and is commonly served on a plate next to pork, greens and cornbread or hush puppies. Recipes vary, but smoked meats, okra, corn, beans and vinegar normally find their way into the stew which should carry a distinct smokiness as well. Burgoo is Brunswick stew's cousin to the northwest. Commonly associated with Kentucky, it's another thick stew made with a variety of meats and veggies and served with barbecue.

Creamed corn is the most popular way of serving corn, but grilled, smoked or deep-fried corn on the cob is also common. Similar to mac 'n cheese, a restaurant's creamed corn could either belong in a school cafeteria or be an absolute delight with a combination of heavy cream, buttermilk, and quality cheeses over freshly smoked or grilled corn.

Fried okra is one of my favorite sides. Most restaurants claim to make everything from scratch, but, when you pry deeper, you learn that this isn't always true. Okra is typically the first item on which to call their bluff. Okra can be difficult to source, has a limited harvest and does not grow in all parts of the country, but give me another made-from-scratch side rather than frozen okra.

While most okra recipes are similar, I found one that absolutely stood out above the rest in, of all places, Salt Lake City.

In some parts of the country, people think serving fries with barbecue is crazy. Fries are for burger joints, they say, not barbecue. No city combines fries with barbecue like Kansas City where, not only are they offered almost everywhere, they are often the best selling side dish. I enjoy fresh fries, especially with a dash of rub on them, as a way of tasting my way through a variety of barbecue sauces.

Sweet potatoes can be found everywhere, but are most commonly served with barbecue in the South. Sweetened, baked purees with or without nuts are quite common, but sweet potato fries are not hard to find. Unfortunately, most sweet potato fries are the frozen and fried type instead of the easy-to-make, salubrious baked sweet potato fries.

Barbecue spaghetti can be found as a main dish, but is often served as a side. Few places outside Memphis serve barbecue spaghetti, but I found it as far away as South Dakota (in a Memphis-style restaurant). The cliché with barbecue spaghetti is that people either love it or hate it. I don't hate it, but you won't catch me ordering it.

Hash 'n rice hasn't made a name for itself in the barbecue world far from South Carolina, but it deserves a mention as it is distinctly tied to barbecue in the Palmetto State. Hash is a thick, savory, meat-heavy sauce that can be taken a number of flavor directions. South Carolinians may have my head for it, but the yellowish hue over white rice reminded me most of a thicker South Asian curry.

Cornbread, hushpuppies and white bread are sometimes considered sides and sometimes considered garnish. Cornbread styles range from dense, grainy, greasy skillet cornbreads to light, sweet and cake-like. I tend to prefer the latter, but appreciate the former when it's done authentically. Corn bakes and corn puddings fit somewhere between this category and the creamed corns.

Hushpuppies replace cornbread in the Carolinas. White bread is the starch of choice for Texas and Kansas City. Hefty piles are often thrown on trays or whole bags left on the tables for customers to have at their liking.

Pickles are generally considered garnish, but fried pickles can be a side or appetizer. It's a small thing, but I appreciate a restaurant making the effort to pickle their own pickles or find them from a local supplier. The most interesting pickle I found was the Kool-Aid pickles at Lillie's Q in Chicago. It was a pinkish pickle that tasted just as you might expect a pickle marinated in cherry Kool-Aid to taste.

Plenty of other sides are to be enjoyed with barbecue including baked potatoes, garden salads, veggie medleys, cucumber and tomato salads, cheesy broccoli bakes, asparagus, rice and beans, dirty rice, and deviled eggs.

Dessert

Dessert may be the most undercapitalized portion of the menu for barbecue restaurants. Dessert is an easy upsell of items that typically hold well. Barbecue is comfort food and what's more comforting than a homemade cookie, brownie or slice of pie?

While only a fraction of barbecue restaurants serve dessert, a few have what is essentially a separate dessert business attached to their barbecue restaurant. 4 Rivers Smokehouse in Orlando has a full bakery featuring decadent desserts and Brushfire BBQ Co. in Tucson has a full ice cream shop churning out interesting flavors like Whiskey Pecan and Habanero Orange. Some restaurants offer a free dessert bar with cobblers and ice cream available. Chris Carby of Branch BBQ in Austin made the root beer float obsolete with his homemade root beer flavored ice cream. The most commonly found desserts at barbecue restaurants are pie, carrot cake, banana pudding, bread pudding, cookies and ice cream. Some restaurants make desserts in-house, some source from local bakeries and some serve commercial products right out of a box. Like anything, quality is all across the board. Some of the best desserts, like the cheesecake at Sweet Rack Rib Shack, came from restaurants where the owner or chef had a background in fine dining. Others, like the carrot cake at Enoch's in Springfield, Missouri, are old family recipes.

Styles of restaurants

There is no one-size-fits-all barbecue restaurant style. "Seasoned" barbecue trailers and food trucks are on one end of the spectrum. These may be permanently parked or out on the prowl. Some of these trucks are run by newbies, others by old barbecue hands. The "10,000 Hour Rule" is an almost magical barrier for becoming an expert in a chosen craft and I think it applies to barbecue. People who spend 60 hours a week over a smoker for 40 years have a level of understanding impossible to learn from books or classes. At the other end of the spectrum, there are white tablecloth barbecue restaurants with professional service, extensive drinks lists and the choicest of ingredients. At least 10 of my Top 100 restaurants are run by chefs with professional culinary training. Their food knowledge, deft understanding of flavors and business acumen work together to create a great barbecue experience.

Different varieties of restaurants can be found in all corners of the country, but I noticed distinct regional variation. The Carolinas have more full-service restaurants, but this does not mean they are nicer. You can place an order for a slaw-topped pulled pork sandwich and a side of hush puppies for $5 with many waitresses. Kansas City has more counter service than other regions. The market (or cafeteria) style of service is rarely seen outside Texas, unless at a Texas-style restaurant.

The popularity of barbecue has grown tremendously over the last 15 years. This can be attributed to the rise of food television, growth of barbecue competitions, increased relocation and travel, and, I believe, a rise in the quality of barbecue restaurants. Each city has an old guard of barbecue restaurants and a rash of newcomers as well. One particular strain of these newer restaurants is what I deem the "Hipster Whiskey Bar." These places make their money from alcohol, but think they should serve some kind of food since they have a kitchen. They have the notion of barbecue being easy, but subpar barbecue is often what you find at these places. It's easy to make passable barbecue. If your focus isn't fully on the food, though, you will not achieve great barbecue.

A great meal is enhanced by a great drink. Whether it be a local craft beer in St. Louis, Portland or Ashville; a Shiner or Lone Star in Texas; a local bourbon in Appalachia; or a smoked cocktail featuring beef bouillon, bacon or boiled peanuts in a metropolitan area, barbecue is better with a drink in hand. I do not, therefore, deride barbecue restaurants with a quality drinks list, but I always want to know if these restaurants care more about the "bar" or the "cue" in barbecue.

It seems license plates, beer signs, mounted wildlife, signed 8X10's of pseudo-celebrities and other kitschy accoutrements must be prepackaged with smokers. For instance, I visited a hillbilly-themed restaurant in California complete with the pink-leopard-print-thong-and-two-PBR-cans-on-a-hanger "Hillbilly Dream-

Catcher." Exceptions to the barbecue cliché decorating schemes can be found, such as the pirate-themed barbecue restaurant I visited in Indiana. North Dakota marketing efforts reached a new low with an alien-inspired version of Chuck E. Cheese claiming to sell the "Best Ribs in the Entire Universe."

Origins of restaurants

After many years as a brick mason in Tuscaloosa, Alabama, Big Daddy Bishop needed a new career. He couldn't decide, however, whether he should open a mortuary or restaurant. After praying for direction one evening, God told him, in a dream, to open a restaurant. I like to think that with Dreamland, he opened both a restaurant and mortuary for pigs.

The origins of most restaurants are not quite this exciting, but I enjoyed hearing stories of the perils and colorful characters behind many restaurants. The dining room at Northwest Arkansas' Fred's Hickory Inn was previously a dormitory for a church camp turned hippy commune. LC of LC's Bar-B-Q in Kansas City started cooking over a fire made in a truck rim topped with hog wire. Every restaurant has its own story, people, struggles and successes, but many restaurants share similar paths. I'll list them in the order I found most common.

First, many restaurants were birthed out of a barbecue competition team. It started with someone buying or receiving an inexpensive backyard smoker. This person smoked a pork butt every couple months, then smoked ribs, brisket, sausages or chicken almost every weekend. After a few years of tinkering in the back yard and receiving endless praise from friends and family, our backyard smoker entered a barbecue competition. He most likely got smoked, but met some nice people, picked up a few tips and left determined not to finish in last place again. After improving his technique and knowledge over a few years, he left his job in insurance, auto repair, teaching or software (all actual examples from my visits) to start a new career.

Second, and somewhat similar, are the people who started as backyard smokers and moved to catering. When friends, family and neighbors tasted their barbecue, they asked them to cater their kid's birthday party, the neighborhood block party, a club fundraiser or a church dinner. One job led to another and before long, they faced a decision to turn down catering business or leave their day job. I'm sure many choose to remain in their careers, but the people who now own restaurants chose to go out on a limb and see what happened.

Many of these owners catered for five or ten years before opening a brick and mortar restaurant. Catering is often 20-35% of a restaurant's revenue and is, by far, the most profitable part of the business. Feeding 100 or 1,000 people off-site is much faster, easier and cheaper than taking care of 100 or 1,000 people in your restaurant. Some barbecue folks have closed their dining room space and only cater. One place in Colorado will gladly serve you a plate of food, but you had better call ahead to make sure they are at the restaurant and smoking. If they are out catering, the doors will be locked.

Some of my favorite restaurants were started by chefs with backgrounds in fine dining. Some of these chefs were tired of the culture, competition and snobbery of the fine dining community and wanted to do something more laid back and down to earth. Some left the South to work in restaurants in New York, San Francisco, Seattle or Chicago before deciding it was time to go home. By returning to their family roots, they also returned to their culinary roots.

Others saw an opening in the competitive restaurant market for barbecue. Despite the growing popularity of barbecue over the last 15 years, many major markets did not have great options for barbecue. Some, I found, still do not! There is certainly something to be said for the untrained barbecue hand who has learned all he knows from word of mouth and endless hours over a smoker, but I found barbecue folks with backgrounds in fine dining to be able to create great all-around dining experiences. Some chef-owned barbecue restaurants survive on restaurant management expertise alone. In a city that doesn't have great barbecue, this can work. The chef-owned restaurants that made the Top 100, however, have devoted the time and tinkering necessary to create amazing smoked meats.

A surprising number of barbecue restaurants have been opened by people laid-off from unrelated businesses. With many of these restaurants opening between 2008 and 2010, they entered the market at a difficult time. The ones I met weathered the storm and are optimistic about the future. The story would often go like this: "I had been with my company for 20 years until they decided to replace the old guys with younger folks to save money. My wife asked me what I really enjoyed in life and the answer was barbecue."

Since people generally ate out less during the economic woes that began in 2008, most said this was a difficult time for their businesses. Depending on the menu and area, though, barbecue can be one of the more reasonably priced food options and some actually thrived during the economic downturn. Some barbecue restaurants had patrons leave their $7 lunch for the $4 fast-food next door, but others saw an increase in business from people opting for their $10 barbecue dinner over the more expensive steakhouse across town.

Another group of barbecue owners began their path to ownership without realizing it. A teenager would start washing dishes, bussing or serving and find themselves as the manager a few years later. Sometimes the owner retired and sold the business to an employee or sometimes the employee decided to strike out on their own after learning how to drive in someone else's car.

Some barbecue restaurants are opened by local restaurant management groups. These are generally not chains, but a restaurateur, possibly working with a group of investors, will have a number of concepts around town. These often produce successful, popular restaurants, but I found the quality of barbecue to be mixed as the focus is often more on making money at the bar or creating a trendy atmosphere than making great barbecue.

One of my favorite stories from the trip is that of an Indian man who moved to Kansas City for medical school. He passed Gates everyday on his way to class and always wondered what was so special about the place that people would line up outside to wait for food. One day, curiosity got the best of him and our vegetarian friend went inside to check it out. He ordered a plate of barbecue and that was the end of his vegetarianism. Today he owns a barbecue restaurant.

Many people have barbecue restaurants because it's the family business. They grew up at the restaurant, started working before they were legally of age and it's simply all they know. Some go off to school or try their hand at another career before the restaurant pulls them back. Sometimes there is a drop in quality when a new generation takes the keys to the smoker and sometimes there is improvement and needed change.

The family aspect of barbecue leads to the observation that barbecue kitchens may be the cleanest in America. I don't mean they have the best scores from the health inspectors or are fastidious with hygiene – some are, some aren't, just as you would find in any group of restaurants. The family aspect of barbecue, concentration in conservative parts of the country, less stressful kitchens due to preparation differences and not having such a structured career ladder make barbecue kitchens, on the whole, much more family-friendly than the drug-fuelled, hyper-sexualized New York fine dining kitchens of Anthony Bourdain's writings. Barbecue has as much testosterone as any genre of food and dependence issues certainly exist, but the professional experience is different.

I often heard stories of the importance of the regular presence of ownership. When owners are not around, the stories go, quality control loosens, employees do not live up to the same standards and the easy way becomes more attractive than the right way. An owner doesn't necessarily need to man the smoker, take orders and make every plate for the restaurant to work – it most certainly would not work with this arrangement. An owner who rarely shows up, lives in another state or isn't passionate about barbecue, though, rarely owns a great barbecue restaurant. Whatever the owner's role, successful restaurants (serving great barbecue and making money) always have a trusted, long-serving management team with skin in the game. Many successful restaurants have given equity to pitmasters and managers. They not only show up and do their job well, they tell the teenage busboy to be say "Sir and Ma'am" because it makes a difference to their bank accounts.

Restaurants where the owner runs everything himself and pays the staff minimum wage may make more money in the short term, but restaurants that succeed in the long run take care of their people, reward their team and empower their staffs. When this happens, it isn't of great importance whether the owner is present the day you visit. A great owner will have his team operating the same way with or without him. The ideal owner role is predominantly accountability and oversight, not total disengagement or micromanagement. Don't be the Jerry Jones of barbecue owners.

We all have a restaurant or bar we love to an inexplicable, illogical level. This place really isn't that great, but we love it. It isn't just a business; it's "my place." One owner told me he isn't trying to be the best barbecue restaurant in town, he's trying to be people's favorite. Rather than enjoy the back-patting of local food writers or the cooing of barbecue experts (overweight, bearded men in overalls), he wants to see the same families week after week. He wants the kids to visit during Christmas vacation when they return home from college. When these kids have their own families, he wants the new kids brought up in his restaurant. It's a concept that will probably build him a loyal customer base and profitable restaurant.

I still hope it doesn't have to be one or the other: best or favorite. It's difficult to achieve either, though, and nearly impossible to do both. If you are trying to attract families you might have a kids menu, a different atmosphere and try to cut corners on food costs to keep menu prices down which would all affect the goal of being the "best." I think it's an interesting concept and appreciate that they have an understanding of their goals and identity.

When a restaurant owner asks for my thoughts and advice, my first two questions are "What do you want to be?" and "Who do you want to reach?" Like most endeavors in life, the answers to these two questions should direct action. Too many barbecue restaurants simply want to be "barbecue restaurants." These don't do particularly well. A restaurant needs focus and identity.

Competition barbecue

Barbecue competitions have only increased the popularity of barbecue – especially in areas outside traditional barbecue country. First, competitions get more people involved in barbecue. One restaurant owner with experience as a chef made his first leap into barbecue at a competition. He entered with confidence because of his training and accomplished culinary career, but left with his tail between his legs after finishing dead last. This started a quest to become the best in barbecue which, after opening a barbecue restaurant, made his food that much better. Second, and related, competition barbecue encourages the barbecue community to continue to learn, adapt and improve. Hundreds of factors play into the food given to judges and much of the innovation in barbecue restaurants was first pioneered on the competition circuit. Competitions bring people together which also fosters the spread of these improvements.

Many barbecue competition teams travel extensively and see the same opponents weekend after weekend, year after year. This has created a fraternity and what appears to be an incredibly supportive community. I found examples of bad blood between cross town restaurants stemming from divorces or falling outs between partners or pitmasters, but most rivalries are good-natured differences of opinion about food. Many restaurant owners are proud of their barbecue lineage and received training, advice and even recipes from cross town "rivals" when opening their restaurants. These friendships extend outside the restaurants as people donate their time, talent and treasure to organizations such as Operation BBQ Relief where owners provide plates of barbecue to disaster areas such as tornado hit Joplin, Missouri, and Hurricane Sandy wrecked New Jersey.

The growth in popularity of barbecue within a city or region is good for everyone, even if there is increased competition. Barbecue creates conversations, disagreement and buzz. Black's Barbecue is the oldest single family-owned barbecue restaurant in Texas and is my favorite in Lockhart. I asked Barrett Black what happened to Black's and Lockhart in recent years with all of the attention, press and buzz surrounding the barbecue scene in Austin. He said business had never been better and referenced the old adage that a rising tide lifts all boats. Since my visit, Black's expanded with a location in Austin.

My 365th barbecue restaurant visit was at Salt + Smoke in St. Louis which opened a few months prior to my visit. I thought it a nice bookend to the project to visit a restaurant which was not in St. Louis when I started the Barbecue Rankings Tour there one year earlier. St. Louis has plenty of barbecue restaurants and my first question to Tom Schmidt, Owner of Salt + Smoke, was simply "Why open another barbecue restaurant in a city with so many of them?" He didn't see the St. Louis market as oversaturated and pointed to his own street, the bustling Delmar Loop. Within a few blocks, one can grab a burger at six places, taco at six restaurants, Asian at eight, or pizza at seven restaurants with Middle Eastern, Greek and other varieties in the mix as well. Shouldn't there be at least one barbecue restaurant in the middle of all of this? I think he's right.

Many of the restaurant owners and pitmasters I met are involved in competition barbecue, but it was a minority. Many simply do not have the time to get away from their restaurants or are too invested in the day to day operations to step away during a busy weekend. Many found competition barbecue to be their gateway into the barbecue world, but have since stopped competing. I found the quality of restaurants owned by decorated competition teams to vary. In some cases, the drive to be the best and commitment to excellence clearly carries from the competition boxes to the restaurant plates. In other cases, I found some owners over-occupied with competitions to the point that the restaurant was an afterthought.

A wall laden with trophies isn't a bad sign when you walk into a barbecue restaurant, but it doesn't always foretell a great meal. In addition to the distraction factor, some of those trophies are the equivalent of college intramural flag football awards rather than the Vince Lombardi trophy of barbecue. Thousands of barbecue restaurants in America serve "Award Winning" or "Grand Champion" barbecue. See if they won with chili at the Third Baptist Church of Challis, Idaho's, annual chili cookoff or for ribs at *Memphis in May*.

Competition barbecue has very stringent guidelines on what constitutes a winning box. Debates over competition standards remind me of the Common Core discussions in education. On one hand, people argue that there needs to be a standard by which everyone is judged. Others argue that these standards inhibit competitors from making their best barbecue. After all, the diversity of flavors and styles is part of what makes barbecue great.

Competition barbecue rules have set artificial ideals for the perfect bites of barbecue. Competition winning barbecue might actually not be anyone's favorite. Most people, for example, prefer ribs that are more tender than competition ribs which, by protocol, require a tug to remove the meat from the bone. Others, myself included, bemoan the trend towards making everything as sweet as possible. This is one reason I prefer to go to restaurants. The public is the judge. We judge with our feet, wallets and taste buds and are not tied to someone else's idea of what great barbecue should be.

Some restaurants claim to serve "competition quality" barbecue. The food they serve to guests, they say, is exactly what they would serve to a judge at a competition. I appreciate a restaurant striving to this ideal, but it simply is not possible. Most competitors use different smokers, woods, qualities of meats, etc. at the restaurants than in competitions, while the sauces and rubs are often the same. Some restaurants replicate their competition 'cue better than others, but babysitting one brisket or rack of ribs is very different from producing 25 briskets and 50 racks for a day at the restaurant. While I think competition barbecue is great for the barbecue world, it has no bearing on my rankings. If a restaurant owned by a famous competitor isn't serving great barbecue, it didn't make the list.

Chains

I appreciate knowing what to expect when staying at a chain hotel. The corner hardware store often has weird hours and limited selection so I frequent Lowe's or Home Depot. I prefer a computer manufactured in an Apple or Dell factory in China to a local high school kid building computers in his parents' basement. When it comes to food, however, I eschew national chains.

I don't begrudge the big barbecue chains for running successful businesses, and the food from Famous Dave's or Dickey's is actually better than many of the alternatives outside barbecue country. A chain restaurant in a strip mall of the inner level of suburban hell can never, however, define barbecue. I heard multiple times in Minnesota and Wisconsin that the original Famous Dave's, which burned down in 2014, was absolutely incredible. An Oklahoman told me the original Rib Crib in Tulsa was unbelievably delicious. People raved about Red, Hot & Blue back in the day and Dinosaur BBQ is still the biggest barbecue name in the Northeast. From hearing the talk surrounding these four chains, had I created this list 20 years ago, they may have been some of my favorites. If I undertake this project again in twenty years, I expect many of my favorites to have opened scores of restaurants. They may make a lot of money, but they may also lose the qualities that made them great.

As restaurants gain followings and build reputations, there is pressure to expand, grow or franchise. Some refuse and stick to their original one or two restaurants. Some that multiply are able to do it well and maintain the consistency of their product, service and experience. Others grow poorly and live off the reputation of the original restaurant. I visited a handful of the bigger regional chains on the Barbecue Rankings Tour, but none of the biggest chains made the list. Some of the Top 100 have 3-5 locations and a couple have more, but the vast majority have one or two locations.

I visited Kansas City early on the Barbecue Rankings Tour. One of my favorite spots was a newer place called Jon Russell's. It had been open for less than a year, and, while its suburban setting wasn't my thing, I found incredible barbecue. During my ten ensuing months of gallivanting around the country exploring barbecue, Jon Russell's expanded the original restaurant and opened three more locations. I made an unannounced visit to one of the newer locations at the end of my tour to see if they still lived up to that great first barbecue experience. I was pleased with the meal and believe they were able to replicate well. If a restaurant has multiple locations, I made it a point to try the original as often as possible. I expect that quality might drop at some chain's newer locations. Keep that in mind as you plan your road trips.

My number one spot in the rankings is a little mom-and-pop operated trailer. I'm not the only one to give them positive press, but in some ways I hate to do so. As a little place like this gets attention, it no longer remains a hidden gem. Even with a single location, some restaurants are able to transform and handle success well, others are not. To me, Arthur Bryant's is fine, not great. I've heard from a number of people that it isn't what it used to be 10, 20 or 30 years ago. I would hate to see my favorite places go the same way, but, if this is to be the case, I'm sure new alternatives will fill the void.

Food Trucks

Trailers, parked food trucks with flat tires or open air restaurants are nice ways to describe barbecue shacks. These have advantages over traditional brick and mortars, like lower overhead costs and fewer regulations, but have drawbacks such as weather dependency and a lack of storage and prep space. Mobile food trucks, however, are a completely different animal. Mobility can expose you to more people, but make it inconvenient for loyal customers to track you down. Mobile trucks rely on public spaces for guest seating and are often competing against a row of food trucks.

You can buy just about any kind of food out of food trucks and barbecue is no exception, although most of it is not great. Some of these food trucks are extensions of established barbecue brands. A few owners told me their food trucks are not extremely profitable, but great for marketing. Others told me the trucks are cash cows. When they take the truck to events or gatherings, they sell as much as they can store in the truck – often at a markup from the prices at the restaurant. Other restaurants operate trucks as part of their catering services. The mobile kitchen and prep area make serving off-site easier. Finally, some barbecue businesses operate solely as food trucks.

When brick and mortar restaurants were available, I always opted for these. I did, however, visit about a dozen mobile food trucks in my year of barbecue. Some I tracked down to wherever they happened to be that day. Some had a rotation where they would be at the same location every Monday, the same location every Tuesday, etc. I visited a couple of food trucks who made agreements with security-conscious companies to provide an on-site food option. This kept fewer people from coming in and out of the secured campus and gave the truck, in some ways, a captive audience.

Barbecue is especially challenging to serve well out of a food truck, because barbecue can not be prepared to order like a burger or taco. A few food trucks have smokers built directly onto the truck or trailer, but most smoke off-site. These businesses smoke overnight, load the food into the truck's warmers and take off for the day. While there is value to letting meat rest, it's a challenge to hold it well over any length of time. Nevertheless, I think this is another area where we will continue to see growth in barbecue.

Gimmicks

Like any business, the barbecue world has its gimmicks. Some are innocent marketing schemes; some involve deception. Eating challenges are particularly popular. The most common of these involves a platter piled high with pork, brisket, chicken, slaw, beans, sauce, pickles, fries, potato salad and whatever else needs to leave the kitchen. Another common gimmick is to have an empty smoker near the road pumping out smoke. The smoke trail, it is argued, is an advertisement referred to as "a sign for the nose." One such restaurant spreads their scent through the neighborhood with a big, wood-burning smoker and uses an oven inside for the food. The owner told me it was much more work using the big smoker. Don't worry...they aren't in the Top 100.

Some restaurants could smoke more of a particular product, but find greater value in saying they are sold out. This generates buzz, hits people squarely in the FOMO sweet spot and makes people believe this item is worth the travel, inconvenience and wait. Most restaurants that plan to sell out do not intentionally short an item, but a few do.

When I inquired about one restaurant's semi-famous touch with ribs, the owner confided it didn't enhance the food, but was a marketing gimmick. Another trick is to throw in one stick of apple wood, or whichever strain they believe to be publically pleasing, with the cheapest wood they can find – like the framing from the nursing home torn down due to asbestos concerns - in order to call their barbecue "apple smoked." These kinds of things, however, are the exceptions. Most barbecue restaurants are straight forward, honest, and view business as the trade of a customer's hard-earned money for a carefully prepared, generous meal.

Every Man's Dream: A Day in the Life

"To awaken quite alone in a strange town is one of the pleasantest sensations in the world. You are surrounded by adventure. You have no idea of what is in store for you, but you will, if you are wise and know the art of travel, let yourself go…"

-   Freya Stark

I am self-diagnosed with a severe and very real medical condition called itchy feet. I like to be on the move. I like to see, experience, taste, learn and know. I like to travel. I'm sure many people have visited all 50 states within one year, but I only made it to 48. Nevertheless, this project provided an opportunity to see, taste, experience and learn about the people, culture, communities and food from all corners of our country.

America is big. In one year, I drove 31,000 miles and flew to eight destinations. I slept on 35 beds, 16 couches, two floors, one overnight bus and camped in seven states. I rarely slept in the same place more than a week.

One of the great joys of the trip was exploring new-to-me parts of the country. I visited national treasures such as Yosemite, Yellowstone and Mt. Rushmore. I explored big cities like Boston and Portland as well as tiny towns like Prattville, Alabama, and Pecos, Texas. I had the freedom to watch a Cardinals Spring Training game in Jupiter, Florida, walk along Cocoa Beach the next day and visit Disney World the following day. I bellied up to a dive bar in Cheyenne, Wyoming, for a Bud Light and had a cocktail in a trendy New York bar.

From South Carolina to Seattle, Memphis to Minneapolis, Dallas to Denver, I visited friends and family scattered throughout the country. In places where I did not know anyone, I sometimes used AirBnB, found an inexpensive hotel or camped. I often, however, used Couchsurfing.com. Couchsurfing.com pairs those with an open couch, or spare bedroom, with travelers. It's an excellent way to meet people and explore a city through the eyes and experience of a local. My first experiences with Couchsurfing were in Europe and I considered these to have been friendly, educational and culturally insightful.

I Couchsurfed with people all over the country. This provided enough stories for another book. I'm going to highlight four of my stays just to give you a taste of the experience and glimpse into my year of barbecue travels. On Couchsurfing, you create a personal profile similar to a Facebook page and message people through the website. I emailed someone in Philly and asked if I could stay with him for a night while I was in town. He invited me to stay, and said he and his roommates were hosting a party that Saturday night. I wasn't opposed to a party. We met late in the afternoon after I had visited a few restaurants and he joined me for my final restaurant stop of the day. The barbecue was disappointing, but we headed back to his house to prepare for the party.

Despite my adventurous ways, the rule-obeying Navy man in me wins out as I have never had anything to do with illegal substances. This was not the case with the people at this party. As I gave a few travel tips to a couple soon off to Thailand, a young, thin man with darkened eyes walked over and joined the conversation. He had overheard our discussion and shared that he had recently returned from a two week trip to Asia. After a discussion of his route, the conversation returned to sights to see and things to do in Bangkok. We discussed Chatuchak, the world's largest outdoor market, and I commented that one can see and find just about anything imaginable there. The newest member in our conversation casually shared that he dropped acid while visiting this market. He and his travel companion packed tabs of acid in tubes of Chap Stick for their trip. The pair forgot about the drugs during their first week in China, but remembered the Chap Stick acid upon arrival in Thailand. Naturally, they decided to drop acid at the Chatuchak Market. This is the point when I thought to myself, "Who are you - person who forgets smuggling drugs into countries where, if caught, the penalties are decades of detention?" It's one thing to make the decision to smuggle drugs. It's another thing to be so carefree about the consequences of getting caught you forget the acid in your carry-on. As the party raged on, I went to the basement to sleep on the floor.

Another Couchsurfing experience of note happened in El Paso, Texas. Here I was, traveling the country consuming enough meat to feed a small village, and I stayed with a family of vegans in Texas – bumper stickers on Priuses and all. They were extremely kind and frequently hosted Couchsurfers. The family shared stories of hosting travelers who rode bicycles across America or took thousand mile treks on foot. They were kind enough to prepare "Vegan Brisket" for dinner which was soy product covered in a red, tomato-based sauce. It was surprisingly enjoyable, but not brisket.

The only negative experience I had with Couchsurfing in my many stays across the US happened in California. The man I stayed with had hundreds of positive references as he hosted quite frequently when he lived in Asia. I met him at a time, however, when he was mentally unstable. Within minutes of meeting, he shared that he was having dreams of suffering in hell and killing his best friend's parents. He broke down a couple of times and I felt more concern for him than fear for myself. I thought about bailing, but decided to stay and woke up the next morning without finding myself in a garbage bag cut into a hundred different pieces.

Finally, on the other end of the spectrum, I had a wonderful visit with someone in Salt Lake City. The gentleman I stayed with is divorced and works from his spacious home, enjoys showing off his city and genuinely appreciates making new friends. He gave me the Salt Lake City tour that included the Mormon highlights, businesses of interest and local parks. One night, after visiting a barbecue restaurant together, we made our way to the Piper Down Public House. It was Bingo night, and, although we never won the first prize of gift cards to the pub, I hit bingo for a mystery prize. Two girls, however, also hit bingo on the same number. When the host announced that a dance-off would determine the winner, one girl immediately took her seat. She could sense my prowess on the dance floor.

The announcer played a techno version of Mozart (yes, you read that correctly) and we were off. My early-twenties, cute, Asian competitor had dance moves you expect to see in the 21st century, but I thought an exuberant minuet would be appropriate considering the music. A minuet needs a partner and when a member of the crowd refused my hand, the announcer, who clearly weighed over 300 pounds, obliged. I won the applause vote and was presented with the mystery prize. It was intended as a joke, but I was as pleased to receive a 1960's hardback copy of

Julia Child's *The French Chef Cookbook* as I was to boast about winning a dance-off to techno Mozart in a Salt Lake City Irish pub.

My vehicle, travel companion and home for the year was my 1999 Subaru Outback I lovingly call "Subie." Subie started the year with over 130,000 miles, so I expected to have a few mechanical hiccups along the way. The first occurred in Texas as I sputtered my way into a repair shop in Houston. The second occurred in Des Moines when the clutch cable snapped and stranded me in the middle of a street. Event number three was the most costly. I was on Highway 10 in southern Arizona when my check engine light flickered and caught my eye. As I glanced down, I saw my temperature gauge was to the point where if Subie had an ejection seat, I was about to go through the roof. I pulled over and eventually made my way to the little town of Benson. Of all the places to be stranded, Benson, Arizona, would not be near the top of my list. I found a repair shop by 1PM and was told I might get on the road that afternoon. I think the mechanic enunciated a number when quoting the cost of the repair, but all I heard was "All-inclusive trip to the Caribbean."

With hours to burn I wandered around town by foot. I passed a barber shop with an interesting marketing strategy - a misspelled name! The sign read "Johnny's Barber Shop" while the etching on the window read "Johnnie's Barber Shop." As I positioned myself to snap a picture of the opposing signs, the barber strutted outside and proclaimed it would cost $25 to take a picture of his shop. I continued on my way without asking him how he spells his name.

I made my way back to the repair shop at 4PM and an employee from the auto parts shop next door walked over and shouted towards the mechanic "How's it goin', Bill?" Only one word was uttered in response, "Shitty", as he continued to tinker underneath the hood. That wasn't a good sign. Sure enough, I had a night in Benson ahead of me.

A near-toothless, larger woman at the shop, who I guessed to be Bill the Mechanic's wife, offered me a ride to the Days Inn approximately 2 miles away. I gladly accepted. I like knowing the name of whomever I'm trusting behind the wheel of a car. I normally ask cabbies for their name if it isn't posted on an ID card somewhere. Some cabbies seem to appreciate my recognition of their humanity while others appear pestered. I introduced myself as Johnny as we climbed into the older Tahoe and asked for her name. "Lalani" was the response.

"I know a Kalani, but you are the first Lalani I have ever met," I responded.

"Lalani means "Heavenly Flower." That's exactly how I would have described her as well.

As we drove, I inquired about the quality of the Mexican restaurant we passed.

"It's closed, but there's a Denny's up here next to the hotel that's really good."

This is what life is like in a town without a barbecue restaurant. Welcome to Benson, Arizona.

No two days were exactly alike on the Barbecue Rankings Tour, but a snapshot of a single day will provide a picture of my life on the road.

I set out from Bakersfield, California, around 8AM on a September morning, drove an hour to Visalia and found a Starbucks. Starbucks or Panera were nearly daily stops for me. After close to two hours spent posting on the blog, answering emails and scouting future restaurant stops, I left for my first restaurant visit of the day.

During my research, Bravo Farms Smokehouse caught my eye. The website reminded me of Chicago q, a white tablecloth spot I enjoyed in downtown Chicago the previous February. Lunch service at Bravo Farms Smokehouse is a sandwich, wrap and salad line, but dinner is a full-service restaurant and steakhouse.

I emailed back and forth with the General Manager before my visit. I planned to spend the day at Sequoia National Park and said I would visit the restaurant right when they opened. In my mind, this meant 11AM. You can understand my confusion when, upon entering at 11, I was welcomed with "You're early!" The gentleman speaking to me thought I would spend the day in Sequoia and visit Bravo Farms right when they began dinner service at 5PM.

Kendel, a young man exuding optimism, pride and vision, introduced himself and I soon discerned he had read nearly everything on my blog. Throughout our conversation he recalled random bits of information about other restaurants that had since faded into the smoky haze of barbecue restaurant memories inside my mind. This kind of reception was not all that common, but it wasn't rare. Some owners effused the "I looked at a few of the pictures on your blog, but don't value your opinion until you say nice things about me" vibe. Others, like Kendel, binge read the entire blog after I reached out to them. Buttering me up? Possibly. Genuinely excited about barbecue and my project? I prefer to think so.

I toured the grounds, talked through the menu with Kendel and ordered a plate of food. Tri-tip was the must-try meat and I was all too happy to sample it over an abundant bed of greens – it's California. As I chowed down, a sampling of ribs, pork, chicken and slaw was delivered to me. "Are you sure this is for me?" was my question to the waitress who responded with an affirming nod. I found some of it to be quite good, some of it to need some work, but, overall, it was an enjoyable visit.

At 1PM I set off for Sequoia National Park. As I drove through the dry, brown landscape, I had a hard time believing the world's largest tree was just a short drive away. I entered the park and ascended mountain after mountain over scotta spaghetti-like roads. (I'll save you the Google search. Scotta is the opposite of al dente. It's overcooked and flimsy pasta, which would make scotta spaghetti-like roads extra tangled.) I paused at a handful of the scenic views to absorb the scenery, bask in the sun and drink in the fresh mountain air (I was far enough away from LA…).

All over America, I had a knack for finding road construction. I am fully qualified to write *The 100 Worst Road Construction Zones in America*, but decided to write this book first. After negotiating road construction inside Sequoia National Park, I detoured for a short hike to the top of Moro Rock. Hoards of American tourists, mostly geriatric, milled about in the parking lot below the rock. I ascended the paved, railed and short, but steep, path to the rounded top. While American English dominated the airwaves just a few hundred feet below, the only English I heard at the top of the rock was heavily accented. I asked an Englishman with a camera lens the size of my calf to take a picture of me with my camera. He and his wife had matching outfits – tan safari hats; tan, multi-pocketed vests and matching pants that were, you guessed it, tan. The biggest difference I could see between the two was that the lady had an emergency tube of Chap Stick securely affixed to a lanyard around her neck. I don't know if it was there so she could lend moisture to cracked lips at a moment's notice (at the ready like an emergency whistle) or if she just wanted to protect it (for protective purposes like the strap on a camera) or if perhaps she was considering dropping acid at that very moment.

What is it with the range of clothes people wear at National Parks? At one visitor center, you will find someone geared-up for a six month venture into the Amazon as well as someone ready for a night out on the town. It's easy to mock a woman in a dress and heels at a National Park, but, truthfully, a stroll through the visitor center and half mile "hike" around the paved, handicapped-accessible "trail" is less strenuous than a shopping trip to Costco. Six month Amazon guy was the one out of place.

While I'm on the topic of National Park wardrobes, I might as well mention the oddity I noticed with the Rangers' clothing. Park Rangers, as you know, have Smokey the Bear-like, drab, uncomfortable-looking brown and green outfits. One would assume they wear this to fit into their natural surroundings. This is what I noticed them wearing inside the visitors center. When I exited the visitor center, however, I found Rangers in another outfit. The layer underneath was the same uniform, but over this was a garish, bright orange construction worker-like vest. This is the government for you. There was probably an accident at one point by an acid dropping, tan outfit wearing, English septuagenarian who didn't see the camouflaged Ranger and now Rangers everywhere where bright orange vests.

Anyway, back to the top of Moro Rock, which was, as you might recall, a mere few hundred feet from the parking lot. In addition to my English friends, there was a group of French teenage girls (one of whom snuck a cigarette on top of the rock), a German-speaking Swiss family and a Japanese couple. There were no other Americans at the top. Whether due to a lack of desire to climb the stairs or inability to do so, it saddened me not to see my fellow Americans at the top of the scenic parking lot overlook.

After negotiating road construction again, I found my way to the General Sherman Giant Sequoia Theme Park. Once again, I joined gaggles of tourists taking the short, scenic and handicapped-friendly stroll to see the world's largest tree (not the tallest, not the widest, but the largest in terms of mass). Near the tree, I spotted a European woman standing as still as a Sequoia with a video camera recording the words on the information signs. Let's pretend somehow this lady has knowledge that the internet will soon disappear and access to information will be limited. Her forward thinking will not only allow her family to learn about the Sequoia forest, but they will not even have to pause the video to read the entire sign since she got a solid two minutes of uninterrupted filming.

As I walked to the less populated side of the tree, I heard a round, loud woman with a deep Southern accent ask a group of Europeans if they wanted her to "make a picture" for them. I inspected her a bit as she made her way to my side of the tree to snap a few of her roughly 200 pictures of General Sherman. She had knee braces on the outsides of her pants on both knees and upon seeing my notebook, asked if I was a student. Surprised by the question, I simply shook my head. After posing for a few pictures for her friend, she shared her frustration to everyone within earshot about not being able to post the photos to Facebook immediately since her phone did not have reception in the park.

I made my way back to the car and set off for the park exit. When I arrived at the exit, the Park Ranger asked for my pass. I had presented my National Park pass to a Ranger as I entered the park a few hours earlier, so it seemed pointless to show it again. Do they have a problem with people sneaking out of the National Parks and into the US? Is this the illegal immigration they speak of on TV?

I continued to weave my way out of the National Forest toward Fresno. I stopped at a scenic overlook and a newer Subaru Outback pulled in shortly after me. Driving a Subaru in a National Park is like ordering a coffee at Starbucks with at least four qualifiers – such as a vente, sugar-free caramel macchiato with an extra shot, pump of raspberry and whipped cream from the milk of a white, two year old goat – it gives you immediate credibility in your surroundings. What's even better, my Subaru was old, beat up and dirty which made it clear this was not my first foray into nature. I'm no soccer mom drawn to a new Subaru by the safety features and comfortable interior. I'm an outdoorsman…or struggling writer.

I continued to Fresno for the second barbecue stop of the day at Dog House Grill. I had a meeting scheduled with the owner, but some sort of emergency unexpectedly pulled him away. I chatted with his business partner who was also tending bar and tried the tri-tip sandwich, pork sandwich, ribs, chicken, beans, fries and a local beer. Most of what I tried was pretty standard and compared favorably to other California barbecue (which isn't hard to do), but the only thing that really stood out was the bordering-on-jam-sweet and sticky barbecue sauce that I happily added to most of the meal.

The partner behind the bar thought the owner might be on his way, so I waited for half an hour but eventually gave up and left for Starbucks. 250 miles, two barbecue restaurants, a national park, a couple stops for road construction, a few hours of people watching and two trips to Starbucks. That's what I called a day on the Barbecue Rankings Tour.

The 100 Best Barbecue Restaurants in America

I visited 365 restaurants for this project, but only 27% could make the Top 100. I ranked the Top 25 and listed the other 75 by region. Some readers will be disappointed not to see their favorite restaurant on the list. Others will see their favorite listed in the Top 100, but take umbrage with being outside the Top 25. I visited most of the highly acclaimed, storied and talked about barbecue restaurants in America. I also mixed in local favorites, hole-in-the-wall finds and off-the-beaten-path restaurants. It's not that the Top 25 are the great restaurants and the other 75 are ok. Of course, the Top 25 were my favorites, but to be listed as one of the Top 100 Barbecue Restaurants in America means a restaurant proved itself as the best of the best. I had an amazing barbecue meal at each of these restaurants and they all beat historic, venerated restaurants to make the Top 100.

Making consistently excellent barbecue is extremely difficult. On more than a few occasions, I took a bite and heard an owner say "Well, that's not quite as tender as I like it." If I visited these 365 barbecue restaurants again, I'm sure my list would be a little different. I hit some on good days and others on bad days.

I viewed the rankings with this question in mind: If I could only eat barbecue one more time, where would I want to go? This helped weigh restaurants against each other and diversify my list. I came to love Texas barbecue, but, if I had only ten barbecue meals, I would want to enjoy different styles of barbecue. Besides, even if a restaurant doesn't serve my favorite style of barbecue, I can still appreciate food prepared at the highest level of that style. The food I had at Skylight Inn was my favorite of the Carolinas, so it made the Top 10. Number 11 on my list is Black's Barbecue in Lockhart which serves, hell, almost defines Texas-style barbecue. If I could only eat one more barbecue meal in my life and my options were 8th ranked Skylight Inn and 11th ranked Black's, I would choose Black's. Skylight Inn noses it out on my rankings, though, because a few Texas-style restaurants were above it in the Top 10. Each restaurant on the list is viewed in light of the restaurants listed ahead of it.

I'm going to go beyond saying "I can't make everyone happy" and say "I can't make *anyone* happy" with this list. Everyone will disagree with something. Knowing this freed me to create the list as I wanted, not try to produce a list for the approval of the casual barbecue fan or food writing community.

There is no perfect plate of barbecue, only perfect plates of barbecue. I'm borrowing and modifying an analogy from Dr. Howard Moskowitz via Malcolm Gladwell. Dr. Moskowitz tested dozens of varieties of pasta sauce in search of the ideal commercial type. Instead of the perfect sauce, he found people's tastes clustered around different kinds of pasta sauces (ex: chunky, sweet, spicy). In a *TED Talk,* Gladwell told a large group of people that if he tried to create a single coffee to fit everyone's tastes, he would end up with a coffee no one liked. If he could organize the audience into smaller groups based on tastes and preferences, however, he could make a targeted coffee for each group that would make everyone happy.

Rather than view barbecue as a ladder where one plate is a step higher than another, we should view it on a horizontal continuum. Barbecue has so many variables and each of us will cluster in different groups based on our preferences. If we formed groups based on preferred texture of pulled pork, we would have clusters around finely chopped and soft, finely chopped with extra texture (like skin and bark), stringy and completely pulled, chunky or cubed, or maybe some combination of a these textures. We could form clusters based on types of wood, levels of smoke, sweetness, levels of spiciness as well as kinds of spiciness (jalapeno, black pepper, cayenne, habanero, etc.), amount of vinegar, type of vinegar, the list goes on and on. If we put ourselves in clusters for the hundreds of variables in barbecue, we would be in a lot of clusters. These preferences and groupings play into what we like. My tastes are, most likely, not exactly the same as yours. You would have a different list if you visited all 365 of these barbecue restaurants. When you visit 365 barbecue restaurants in a year, I promise to buy your book too.

Expectations are lenses bending how we perceive life. Expectations with food are no different. On one hand, people go into a restaurant like Franklin Barbecue expecting it to be the best they will ever eat. Since they have this expectation, they might talk themselves into believing it is, in fact, the best barbecue they've ever tasted. On the other hand, when expectations are high, they are difficult to live up to. More than a few places on the list came out of nowhere to impress me. My number one spot was a newer barbecue trailer that had not received much praise or recognition before my visit. I didn't have high expectations so it was easy for the expectations to be surpassed – and surpassed greatly in this case. These two tensions (expectations being self-fulfilling and the difficulty of living up to high expectations) probably play out differently in each of us. One person might visit my number one spot and talk themselves into believing it to be the best barbecue to ever touch their tongue while another might visit and, regardless of what they are served, never believe it to be the best barbecue in America because the bar is set unattainably high.

Statistical breakdown of the Top 100

As you might expect, the states with the most restaurants in the Top 100 are Texas (20), Missouri (12), Tennessee (10) and North Carolina (6). Georgia also had six. 28 states plus D.C. had at least one restaurant in the Top 100. Viewed regionally, the South had the most restaurants with 40, the Midwest had 26, Texas (as its own region) had 20, the Northeast (including D.C.) had 8 and the West had 6.

The breakdown is similar within the Top 25. Texas had five, Tennessee had four, Missouri had four, Kansas had two, North Carolina had two and eight states had one. None of the Top 25 came from the West. The Northernmost and Westernmost restaurant in the Top 25 is J.R.'s in South Dakota.

Here they are, The 100 Best Barbecue Restaurants in America!

The Top 25

#1. Kerlin BBQ

Austin, Texas

www.kerlinbbq.com

Established: 2013

Style: Texas barbecue out of a trailer in a central, yet less gentrified, portion of Austin. Live music, yard games and picnic tables.

Wood: Post oak.

What to try: Everything…especially the fatty brisket.

What to avoid: Eating a big breakfast.

My absolute favorite barbecue meal of the year came from a little trailer at 1700 E. Cesar Chavez in Austin, Texas. Bill and his wife Amelis operate a permanently parked trailer in a small lot tucked away from the trendier parts of Austin. When I visited in January, they had only been open for six months and were relatively unknown. Kerlin has received some praise since my visit, but is still an off-the-beaten-path find in the barbecue crazed city of Austin.

I expect Kerlin to be compared to Franklin Barbecue for a long time. Franklin is one of the most celebrated barbecue restaurants in America and the two are only one mile apart. I loved Franklin too – it's a Top 10 place - but Kerlin beat it by just a hair for a couple reasons.

First, the bark. Most barbecue restaurants smoke briskets between 225-250 degrees for anywhere between 6 and 20 hours. Not Bill Kerlin. He smokes prime briskets at the unbelievably high temperature of 400 degrees for 12 hours. I do not understand how he isn't serving lumps of coal, but inside the thick, rich crust you find as tender a brisket as you will find anywhere. Perhaps the outside sears and traps the succulent brisket juice inside. Bill could tell me the briskets are actually from endangered Black Rhinos and he stokes the fire with newborn kittens and I wouldn't care. It's that incredible.

While most barbecue restaurants let brisket rest in a wrap (butcher paper, saran or foil), Bill keeps his on the smoker until they are ready to be carved and served. He starts with a thicker bark than anyone else by smoking at such a high temperature and by not wrapping, serves the crunchiest, tastiest bites of barbecue found anywhere.

In addition to the best brisket in America, Kerlin has incredible ribs, a terrific sauce and quality sides. Free beer (yes, I said free!) can often be found on the weekends. Combine this with live music and yard games and it might be as close to heaven as one can find on Earth.

The trailer is permanently parked at this location and there are a few picnic tables set up under the open sky. Kerlin alone is worth the trip to Austin and I can't say enough nice things about it. It's the best barbecue restaurant in America.

#2. Hometown Bar-B-Que

Brooklyn, New York

www.hometownbarbque.com

Established: 2013

Style: Brooklyn with clear Texas influence. Market-style service, rustic/minimalist interior and a bar you expect to find in Brooklyn.

Wood: White and red oak mix.

What to try: First, the brisket. After that, the beef rib, pork ribs and beans.

What to avoid: Hurricane Sandy. The opening was pushed back six months by the storm.

The New York City barbecue scene has received Texas-sized amounts of press in the last year. Dinosaur Bar-B-Que has long been the biggest name in the Northeast and Blue Smoke did much to bring quality 'cue to the Big Apple in the 2000's. I think Dinosaur is what its name implies and Blue Smoke, while good, is now more accurately described as Southern rather than barbecue. Mighty Quinn's was recently named to "New York City's 100 Best Restaurants" by *Zagat*. Delaney Barbecue has received praise from trusted barbecue writers. Fette Sau has a cult-like following in the young professional, hipster circles of Brooklyn. I visited all of these and others, but to me one restaurant towered over New York – Hometown Bar-B-Que.

Hometown has received plenty of praise in their short existence and is now feeding six thousand people a week. I didn't know this at the time, but Hometown is also the favorite of Northeastern barbecue blogger Gary Goldblatt (www.pigtrip.net). This means something since Gary, over many years, has visited 400+ barbecue restaurants across the Northeast. I believe the high praise is fully warranted as I think it is clearly the best in the Northeast and one of the best in America.

Owner Billy Durney spent much of his life traveling the world as protection for some of America's biggest celebrities. He wanted to spend more time at home and turned his hobby of barbecue into a business. Billy is a big fan of Texas barbecue and it's clear with his signature brisket and beef rib. He studied under storied Texas pitmaster Wayne Mueller and, despite being born and raised in New York, has "BBQ" tattooed inside the outline of the state of Texas on his right calf. The restaurant is set up like a traditional Texas market and decorated with a modern, yet rustic, eye for detail. Situated in an industrial area outside the hustle and bustle of Manhattan, the Statue of Liberty can be viewed from the waterfront just a few blocks away in South Brooklyn. Everything, including barbecue, is a bit more expensive in New York, but I'll go out on a limb here and say that, dollar for dollar, you can't find a better meal in the City.

Billy and his pitmaster, Nester, start smoking at 11PM each night and babysit these meats a few blocks away from the restaurant at their smoking location. You will not find a thermometer near the smokers as Billy and Nester work from feel and sight alone. When the briskets receive the nod of approval the next day, they are wrapped in wax paper and butcher paper to rest before being transported to the restaurant.

Everything but the pickles is made in-house. Although I appreciate house-made pickles, I respect Billy saying that he couldn't make them quite as well as a nearby shop. He wanted the best for his customers, and that meant buying from a local pickle producer.

The brisket is absolutely incredible. This isn't a "well, it's good for not being in Texas" kind of thing. It's right there with Kerlin and Franklin as the best in America. Billy is also quite proud of his succulent beef rib which he refers to as "my soul on a plate." The jerk-inspired ribs were fantastic and the thick beans are some of the best you will find anywhere. Everything at Hometown is top notch. If I hear of you going to New York and not visiting Hometown, you should burn this book and never be allowed to eat barbecue again.

#3. Joe's Kansas City Bar-B-Que

Kansas City, Kansas (3 locations)

www.joeskc.com

Established: 1996

Style: Kansas City. Original location is counter service inside a gas
    station. Crowded, busy, amazing.

Wood: Missouri white oak.

What to try: Ribs, beans, Z-Man sandwich, fries.

What to avoid: Arriving at noon or you will have a nice little wait.

From being named one of Anthony Bourdain's "13 Places to Eat Before You Die" to USA Today's "America's Tastiest Ribs" to the myriad of local awards adorning the walls, Joe's Kansas City (formerly Oklahoma Joe's) is one of the most heralded barbecue restaurants in America. Joe's helped popularize pulled pork in the beef town of Kansas City and the ribs have won national recognition. The Z-Man Sandwich is possibly the most talked about barbecue sandwich in America. The baked beans and fries are top notch and the experience is unlike any other.

One of Joe's famed peculiarities is its location inside a functioning gas station and convenience store, but this isn't quite as rare as you might think. I visited a dozen barbecue restaurants built inside old service stations, but only a couple of them were still operational as service stations. While most of these restaurants served, well, barbecue you might expect from a convenience store, Joe's puts out some of the best barbecue you will ever find.

Why a convenience store? After making the progression from casual barbecue competitors to blossoming catering business, owners Jeff and Joy needed refrigeration space. They transformed a corner fried chicken stand and the liquor store next door into a barbecue counter and commissary. Before long, there was a line out the door.

I recommend the ribs or Z-Man Sandwich which is a pile of brisket, provolone and onion rings on a Kaiser. Be sure to get fries and baked beans. The generous bags of fries are a local favorite and the baked beans will make you wonder how they kept these chunky, Southwest-infused beans warm as they expedited them from a chuck wagon on the Santa Fe Trail.

Get in line. It's worth the wait.

#4. The Granary 'Cue & Brew

San Antonio, Texas

www.thegranarysa.com

Established: 2012

Style: Texas market by day, global by night.

Wood: Live oak.

What to try: Something new and unlike anything you have tasted
before. Oh, and a beer.

What to avoid: Going to a bar or another restaurant for dessert –
The Granary has you covered.

The Granary 'Cue & Brew is not your typical barbecue restaurant,
but it honors barbecue tradition: both by respecting the past and
by moving forward with new barbecue techniques, ingredients,
flavors, textures and dishes. It is unlike any other barbecue
restaurant in America and I loved it.

Lunch is the conventional Texas barbecue experience with market-
style service and offerings of brisket, sausage, ribs, beans, potato
salad, etc. The dinner menu transforms these smoked meats

through inventive dishes combining flavors we associate with barbecue such as black pepper, Texas toast, root beer, pecans, collard greens and pickles with less traditional ingredients such as lentils, eggplant, pomegranate and yuzu. The signature Beef Clod is a perfect example. The thick-cut clod comes from the tough, once popular, but now underutilized, beef shoulder. The clod is framed by a coffee quinoa crunch (quinoa steeped in coffee, dehydrated and flash fried), pickled celery, and an angel food cake-like "cornbread." This is surrounded by a ring of tomato caramel that acts as the barbecue sauce. It tastes as good as it sounds.

The older of the two brothers behind The Granary, Chef Tim Rattray, worked in renowned kitchens around the country before opening The Granary. While the food coming out of his kitchen looks like art, Chef Rattray brings a scientific eye to all of his dishes. Younger brother Alex Rattray is the brewmaster who creates fresh beer only available on-site. The beers on tap during my visit were somewhat traditional, but done well. The seasonal house-made sodas, however, are far more adventurous. Cranberry-Pumpkin was a winter offering and the forthcoming Grapefruit-Szechuan Peppercorn sounded quite interesting.

I had to try the Beef Clod, but I also enjoyed an array of appetizers, other mains and desserts. I spent some time in Asia and the Brisket Ramen (smoked showyu broth, brown ale noodles, onsen egg, 'cue shallots and blackened collard greens) rivals any noodle dish I've had. The barbecue butter that comes with the Texas Toast is inexplicably good. For dessert, my favorite was the Beer & Pretzel ice cream which featured mustard caramel and a pretzel crunch.

The Granary 'Cue & Brew is a barbecue destination. Bring friends and sample a few different dishes. It's different, but I loved it.

#5. 4 Rivers Smokehouse

Orlando, Florida (6 locations)

www.4rsmokehouse.com

Established: 2009

Style: Pulls from everywhere, but Texas presence is strongest. Comfortable atmosphere. Market-style line. Professional bakery in-house.

Wood: Hickory.

What to try: Start with the brisket, end with more brisket.

What to avoid: Eating the tasty desserts at the restaurant. Take them home with you and save more room for brisket.

John Rivers' love of barbecue has everything to do with the phenomenal success of 4 Rivers Smokehouse, but it's the motivation behind this success that really matters. After a journey that included an introduction to brisket at a Texan Thanksgiving, a vow to make the best brisket anywhere, traveling to many of America's most respected barbecue restaurants and years of tinkering, testing, tasting and repeating, it took a little girl with cancer to pull John into barbecue for business.

When the Rivers family received a call offering their thoughts and prayers for their cancer-diagnosed child, they were shaken. It was a wrong number and none of their children had cancer. They knew however, that an unknown family and child somewhere was dealing with this terrible disease. They found the family and John catered a fundraiser for the little girl. Word of the barbecue spread quickly, and, even on their first day of business, 4 Rivers had a line into the parking lot. The line hasn't let up since - for good reason.

4 Rivers, at John's leading, continues to play an active role in the community and supports a number of great organizations - including the Ronald McDonald House which is near and dear to my heart.

I heard about 4 Rivers from a number of barbecue fanatics and restaurant owners preceding my trip to Florida, but, I have to admit, I still wasn't convinced a relatively new barbecue restaurant in Orlando would be that great. I'm happy to say my reservations were thrown out the window after the first bite. Everyone should try the brisket on their first visit (and possibly the next day when you go back for more). It's one of the best briskets you can find anywhere. You will not go wrong with anything on the menu, but the brisket is my favorite and it's the dish that made John Rivers into a barbecue man and created 4 Rivers Smokehouse.

#6. Herman's Ribhouse

Fayetteville, Arkansas

www.hermansribhouse.com

Established: 1964

Style: Dark, woody, college-town ribhouse and steakhouse.

Wood: Hickory and oak.

What to try: Spare ribs, garlic chicken.

What to Avoid: I should tell you to resist the steaks since this is a
barbecue book, but they are exquisite as well.

Herman's Ribhouse is an institution.

Some of the world's biggest business deals happened as Sam
Walton, Don Tyson and J.B. Hunt enjoyed casual evenings
together at Herman Tuck's modest home in Fayetteville,
Arkansas. Herman cooked for these titans of American industry
and eventually the men's wives talked their way into joining for
dinner. Herman turned his house into a restaurant in 1964 and,
today, it's a favorite of locals and celebrities alike.

In 1996, Nick Wright visited a friend in Fayetteville. He stayed,
got a job washing dishes at Herman's and, today, he and his wife
Carrie own the restaurant. They take their responsibility to protect
the legacy of one of America's great barbecue traditions quite

seriously. You will find Carrie at the register with Nick in front of the grill as he keeps an eye on both the front and back door (where most regulars enter).

Nick and Carrie, if not too busy, will offer a baby back and spare rib to any first time visitor. Do not expect this welcoming gesture, however, if you arrive on a college football gameday when the wait might be over two hours.

When asked about signature dishes, Nick had a difficult time answering. Herman's calls itself a "Ribhouse" and many people will not order anything other than ribs. Other customers swear by the steaks. A third group of patrons gush over the garlic chicken. The spare ribs are some of the best you will find anywhere, the steaks are superb and the garlic chicken is some of the best chicken I've ever had. Garlic chicken conjures images of yellow, lemony chicken - not really barbecue. Instead, the garlic sauce at Herman's is dark, rich and the perfect complement to the expertly prepared chicken breast.

Every barbecue lover should make the trip to Fayetteville to experience Herman's rich history, great people, classic atmosphere and mouthwatering dishes.

#7. Franklin Barbecue

Austin, Texas

www.franklinbarbecue.com

Established: 2009

Style: Central Texas. Lunch only with a huge line. Retro interior.

Wood: Post oak.

What to try: Brisket and...brisket.

What to Avoid: Sides. Just eat brisket.

A million places have been dubbed the "Mecca" of something. I will not refer to a dozen restaurants as Meccas of barbecue, but just as there is one Mecca, I will use the analogy once. Franklin Barbecue is today's Mecca of barbecue.

Franklin Barbecue was crowned best in the Lone Star State by *Texas Monthly* and has been featured in everything from the *New York Times* to *Bon Appetite* to *Men's Fitness*. It's Anthony Bourdain's favorite barbecue spot and Aaron Franklin is on TV.

When Franklin Barbecue is brought up in conversations around Austin, the only thing discussed more than the brisket is the wait. I met one Texas restaurant owner who waited in line on multiple occasions, but had yet to try the brisket since it was sold-out when he made it to the butcher block.

I braved the line early one morning and found that nearly everyone in line was a visitor to Austin. Most locals will have a hard time investing four hours of their day to lunch on a regular basis. While it isn't something you want to do often, the line itself is an experience. Meeting people is part of the fun. Tailgating helps the time pass and makes the barbecue even better. The anticipation makes you incredibly hungry which only heightens the experience.

I visited on a "slow" day. It was a Wednesday in January, but when I arrived at 9:15, there were 20 people already in line. By opening at 11AM, there were an estimated 125 people in line. Even if your neighbors in line are grumpy and the weather is terrible, one bite of brisket will make you forget about all your troubles. People often rave about the ribs, sandwiches and sauce at Franklin, but for me it's all about the brisket. It's absolutely incredible.

#8. Skylight Inn BBQ

Ayden, North Carolina
www.skylightinnbbq.com
Established: 1947
Style: Whole hog. Dated wood paneling, tiled flooring and fold-up
    chairs that are oh-so-right for barbecue.
Wood: Oak and hickory.
What to try: The Tray.
What to avoid: Visiting on a Sunday. Closed for business.

Sam Jones is a barbecue celebrity, but it's not because he has done anything inventive. Skylight Inn hasn't changed much over the years and that's part of its charm. Pete Jones, opened the restaurant in 1947, and, during my visit, an older gentleman answered his cell phone by saying "I'm at Pete Jones'." It's a small town restaurant where family names still mean something.

Like the food, the décor hasn't changed much over the years. Like many barbecue restaurants, the walls are filled with signed letters and pictures from celebrities and politicians. Unlike most restaurants, however, the pictures at Skylight Inn are faded hues of yellow and brown since they haven't moved in decades.

The best part about Skylight Inn, other than the food, is watching the preparation of pork right behind the counter. The customer sees it chopped, lightly seasoned, scooped and served. The basic tray of chopped pork is topped with a square of dense, greasy cornbread and another tray of fresh, finely minced, slightly sweet slaw: some assembly required.

The real secret of Skylight Inn's food, in my opinion, is found on the table. The light-red vinegar sauce with black pepper and red pepper flakes is my favorite sauce in America. The Jones family must have had a direct line to hog heaven because this sauce is divine.

#9. Central BBQ

Memphis, Tennessee (3 Locations)
www.cbqmemphis.com
Established: 2002
Style: Nouveau Memphis.
Wood: Hickory and pecan.
What to try: Wet ribs, jerk chicken wings, nachos.
What to avoid: Brisket. It's Memphis, go with the pork.

During my travels, I tried to limit how much I ate at each restaurant. I couldn't help myself, however, at Central BBQ. I think of Central BBQ as the Joe's Kansas City of Memphis. Both were on the cusp of the barbecue restaurant wave, are located in slightly obscure locations in barbecue cities and immediately created a loyal local following. That kind of success in the city of Memphis leads to national attention and high praise. I think Central deserves it.

No barbecue nachos in America are as talked about as Central's. They are simple: chips topped with pulled pork, cheese, barbecue sauce, jalapenos and a dash of rub. Somehow, though, the sum is much greater than the parts as they transform into something truly special.

My meat recommendation has to be the wet ribs. I normally prefer dry ribs, but Central's wet ribs are unbelievable. For your dry rub fix, try the spice-kick-to-the-face jerk chicken wings.

#10. Double J Smokehouse & Saloon

Memphis, Tennessee

www.doublejsmokehouse.com

Established: 2012

Style: Memphis meets the Wild West in this downtown saloon.

Wood: Pecan.

What to try: Ribs, pork steak, mustard sauce.

What to Avoid: The half-rack. Go for the whole.

I did not know what to expect from Double J Smokehouse & Saloon. In a town of storied barbecue restaurants steeped in tradition, Double J's had only been in business two years before my visit and felt more like a saloon in old town Amarillo than a barbecue restaurant in Downtown Memphis. I'm glad I visited, though, because despite being somewhat unheralded, it blew me away.

The pork steak may be unfamiliar to much of America, but if you attend a backyard barbecue in St. Louis, there is a good chance you'll find a pork steak on the grill. As a St. Louisan, I was surprised to see pork steak on Double J's menu and was not prepared for what I was about to taste. While a pork steak in St. Louis is usually grilled, cut with a steak knife and drowned in sauce, Double J's dry-rubbed, slow-smoked pork steak flaked on my fork like a piece of fish. It was a transcendent pork experience. Nothing I tasted in my year of travels surprised me more.

After having my pork steak world turned upside down, we moved on to the ribs. The bourbon glaze on the wet ribs was quite tasty, but the dry ribs were even better. The Texas influence is obvious, but I also loved the mustard sauce. It's a different kind of place than what you typically find in Memphis, but it I think it's some of the best barbecue found anywhere.

#11. Black's Barbecue

Lockhart, Texas (2 locations)
www.blacksbbq.com
Established: 1932 – 5 generations ago
Style: Texas market-style, but has a more comfortable restaurant feel than the other old-school Texas stops.
Wood: Post oak.
What to try: Sausages, some kind of beef.
What to avoid: Filling up. There is more to be had in Lockhart.

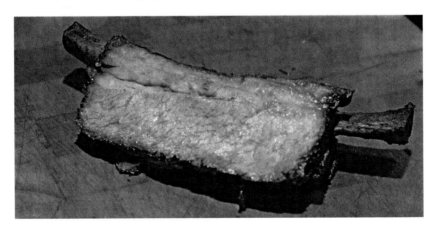

Lockhart has long been considered the heart of Texas barbecue. Some of the famed family names have been around for over a century and this small town of roughly 14,000 people supports multiple large barbecue restaurants. People travel to Lockhart from all corners of the world, but it's just a short drive from Austin.

Black's Barbecue is the oldest single family owned and operated barbecue restaurant in the state. I met Barrett Black, whose great-grandfather opened the restaurant in 1932. Some things have changed over the last eight decades, like Barrett's grandmother coming up with a sauce recipe in the 70's after the "damn yankees" kept asking for it, but much hasn't changed. Barrett recommended the Texas Trinity of brisket, pork ribs and sausage for a first time visitor, but was also quick to highlight the beef ribs since he is particularly proud of these.

I'm always up for a sampler plate, but for me (and LBJ apparently), Black's is all about the sausage. While some places use meat scraps in their sausage, Black's uses quality meat with a 90% beef/10% pork ratio and smokes over aged post oak. Original, Garlic, and Jalapeno Cheddar are always on the menu with a special rotated in (beer sausage during my visit). The Jalapeno/Cheddar sausage is terrific and my favorite sausage in America.

My recommendation for your visit to Lockhart is to visit Black's, Smitty's and Kreuz for a satisfying day of barbecue. All three have their apologists and there are great things about each of them, but Black's was my favorite.

#12. Bogart's Smokehouse

St. Louis, Missouri

www.bogartssmokehouse.com

Established: 2011

Style: Memphis a little further up the Mississippi.

Wood: Apple and cherry.

What to try: Ribs, baked beans.

What to avoid: Nothing. It's all good.

I called St. Louis home for six years, and, before beginning this project, thought Bogart's was the best in town. After visiting 20 more barbecue restaurants in the St. Louis area and finding some new-to-me places that made the Top 100, I still have a thing for Bogart's.

Bogart's is located in historic and fun (how often do those go together?) Soulard. The line is often long, but the friendly staff, quick service and buzz keep the wait from becoming an annoyance. Owner Skip Steele is a no-nonsense kind of guy with a long history in the barbecue business dating back to his youth in Memphis.

Bogart's seems to always have an interesting special, but it's hard to go wrong with the tried and true menu items. The ribs and baked beans are some of the best in America. The apricot glazed ribs are hit with a blowtorch to finish them off with a little caramelization. The beans smoke for hours in the rotisserie-style Ole Hickory Pits smoker and it's like the sky opened as meat drippings fall from heaven into the beans. The sauces, including a pineapple sauce, are interesting and enjoyable. The wings are also hard to beat.

If you want to take your barbecue to go, you can walk a block to iTap and choose from 40 beers on tap and almost 500 different bottled beers. While in Soulard, be sure to visit the Soulard Spice Shop, build your own rub and see what you can do with a rack of ribs or pork butt at home.

#13. Dreamland Bar-B-Que Ribs

Tuscaloosa, Alabama (8 locations)
www.dreamlandbbq.com
Established: 1958
Style: Bib wearin', sauce slatherin', old-school Southern joint that
      wouldn't pass a building safety inspection in most cities.
Wood: Hickory.
What to try: Ribs, sauce, white bread.
What to avoid: The sides. Stick to the tried and true here.

Dreamland started with a dream. Not a lifelong desire to own a barbecue restaurant, but an actual dream. Big Daddy Bishop said that God came to him in a dream and told him to open a restaurant. A few things have changed since 1958, but not everything. Until the 90's, ribs, chips, white bread, beer and soda were the only things served at Dreamland. The question wasn't "What would you like to order?" but simply "How many?" In recent years, the Tuscaloosa location added a rib-meat sausage and a few standard barbecue sides. The newer locations now serve chicken and pulled pork. I can't speak to the quality of the newer locations, but know that the pitmasters at each of these outposts spend time learning at the original Tuscaloosa Dreamland.

Dreamland has a long history, a big reputation and, while many love it, others love to hate it. Some think it's overhyped and not worth its reputation. Others say it's changed and isn't what it used to be. I think it's still a great place to get a plate of barbecue.

Everything is smoked over an open brick pit that utilizes more direct heat than you find at most barbecue restaurants, but the results are still magical. The ribs are perfect and a lot of that has to do with Dreamland's incredible sauce. It's one of my favorites in America and I mopped it up with bite after bite of white bread.

#14. Jon Russell's Kansas City Barbeque

Overland Park, Kansas (4 locations)

www.jonrussellsbbq.com

Established: 2012

Style: Suburban…worth it.

Wood: Apple.

What to try: Burnt ends, Jon Russell sandwich.

What to avoid: The Southwestern-style baked beans.

They are some of the newer kids on the Kansas City barbecue restaurant block, but owners Russell Muehlberger and Jon Niederbremer of Jon Russell's Kansas City Barbeque are familiar faces on the KC barbecue scene. Their reputation includes that little thing of being named Grand Champion of the 1992 *American Royal Invitational*.

If you visit Jon Russell's once, try the burnt ends. They are some of the best in America. The sausage is also good and the Jon Russell Sandwich combines the two of these to create something memorable.

Jon Russell's had not been open for long when I visited in my first month of the Barbecue Rankings Tour. I was blown away. By my twelfth month, they had expanded from one location to four and I wondered if quality had remained the same. I made an unannounced visit to one of the newer locations and tried the burnt ends again. I was not disappointed.

#15. Payne's Bar-B-Q

Memphis, Tennessee

Internets!?! Payne's don't need no stinking internets!

Established: 1972

Style: The holiest of all holes-in-the-wall.

Wood: Charcoal.

What to try: Chopped pork sandwich with slaw.

What to avoid: Bringing an interior decorator.

While some in Memphis consider Payne's Bar-B-Q the best in town, others have never heard of the place. The dark, spartan, smoky interior of Payne's will transport you to another place and time. This austere interior is balanced, however, by the friendly family who has been operating Payne's since 1972.

THE thing to order at Payne's is the chopped pork sandwich with slaw. The bun may be standard, but that's about the only thing I found unremarkable. The iconic neon-yellow mustard based slaw is a perfect pair for the chopped pork. The pork has great texture as it includes some of the tougher charred bits mixed in with the tender, smoky meat. The use of a mild, runny sauce brings the two together for the best barbecue sandwich in America.

#16. Cooper's Old Time Pit Bar-B-Que

Llano, Texas (4 locations)

www.coopersbbq.com

Established: 1963

Style: Hill Country. Pick your meat right off the pits and eat inside
     with real life cowboys.

Wood: Mesquite.

What to try: The Chop, brisket.

What to avoid: Bringing your animal rights activist friend.

Cooper's Old Time Pit Bar-B-Que is another storied and
celebrated barbecue restaurant. It rose from Central Texas favorite
to national notoriety when President George W. Bush declared it
his favorite place for barbecue. Some barbecue purists argue that
Cooper's cowboy style of cooking - meat over heat rather than
indirect smoking - isn't barbecue at all. I'll agree that it pushes the
definition of barbecue, but there is a big difference between
cooking on big, open brick pits and a backyard grill. These pits are
not all that different from some of the old whole-hog places in the
Carolinas. I wouldn't call it grilling, and, since the results are so
tasty, am happy for them to have their place in barbecue.

The atmosphere at Cooper's starts outside. Customers pick their
sausage, pork chop, pork loin, brisket, turkey, pork ribs, beef ribs,
chicken, prime rib or steak right off the pit. A pitmaster carves
your hand selected choices before your eyes. Head inside to pick
up sides, transfer your food to butcher paper, pay and serve

yourself a bowl of free beans. Loaves of white bread and pickled jalapenos await you at the worn, brown picnic tables pushed together for family-style dining. When I sat down, I realized two things. First, I wasn't eating next to businessmen in boots and a hat. Cooper's is a place for real cowboys. Second, there was no music. My ears only heard the clamor of kitchen noises, everyday lunch conversations, football on TV, clacking of silverware and the noisy ice machine that randomly dispenses ice without prompting.

My tray was saddled with pounds of meat masterpieces. Cooper's slogan is "Home of the Big Chop" and their signature meal includes a 2" thick, 1.5 pound pork chop, bacon jalapeno mac 'n cheese, free beans and ice cream over pecan cobbler. I can't argue with that meal, but good luck getting through it.

The pork chop is fantastic and a must-try for a first time visitor, but on your second visit, try the brisket. Due to cooking over a fire instead of in a smoker, it's not quite as smoky as many Texas briskets, but somehow it comes off incredibly tender.

Whatever you think of W's political judgment, I bet you will have a hard time disagreeing with his barbecue judgment when you visit Cooper's.

#17. Puckett's Grocery

Franklin, Tennessee (5 locations)

www.puckettsgrocery.com

Established: 1998

Style: Country grocery turned Nashville-quality live music venue.

Wood: Cherry.

What to try: Ribs, pulled pork.

What to avoid: Lunch, go and enjoy a drink and the music in the
   evening.

As I entered Puckett's, I was immediately met with the warmth
and energy of a restaurant packed with people enjoying live
music, drinks and plate after plate of fine American food.

Puckett's delivers the full restaurant experience, but they take no
shortcuts with their barbecue. I tasted a little bit of everything
with owners Andy and Jan Marshall and particularly enjoyed the
ribs and pulled pork. Many wet ribs apologists love the charred
sweetness of caramelized sauce. Dry rib devotees do not want
anything to mask the flavor of the meat. Puckett's dry ribs satisfy
both camps with their charred sweetness that doesn't overpower
the meat. The pulled pork was tender with a hint of the same
sweetness and smokiness.

#18. Allen & Son Bar-B-Que

Chapel Hill, North Carolina

If Keith Allen didn't need a website 44 years ago, he doesn't need
  one today.

Established: 1971

Style: Pretty much defines North Carolina 'cue.

Wood: Hard hickory.

What to try: Pork with slaw and hush puppies...of course.

What to avoid: Beans.

Keith Allen is the John Wayne of barbecue: rugged, iconic and
traditional. 44 years after opening Allen & Son, he continues
"chasin' the taste." At the green age of 19, Keith took charge of his
family's financial situation and opened Allen & Son Bar-B-Que
with $452 left in his pocket after investing $6,000 in the restaurant.
Little at the restaurant has changed since 1971 and Keith still
works at a pace that would kill most men half his age. Dutifully
shoveling coals into the brick pits every half hour from 2AM on,
Keith carefully tends the pit all night six days a week. On his off
day, Monday, he hauls wood to the restaurant and splits it
himself.

Methods of running a barbecue restaurant, according to Keith, depend on what you are aiming for: easy or good. Many people in the business, he said, are trying to maximize profits or minimize work. He admits there are scores of easier ways to make a living, but he's not in barbecue to find the optimal profit to work ratio.

The chopped pork speaks for itself. It's a favorite of many in North Carolina for good reason. The story, history, ambiance and experience is special, but without great barbecue, it's all for nothing. Luckily, you can find some great pork at Allen & Son.

#19. The Shaved Duck

St. Louis, Missouri
Established: 2008
www.theshavedduck.com
Established: 2008
Style: American fare casual dining.
Wood: Cherry and hickory from Prairieville, MO.
What to try: Burnt ends, bacon, mac 'n cheese.
What to avoid: Meatloaf wasn't bad, but other meats are better.

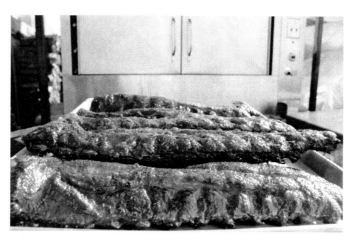

The Shaved Duck is a small, bustling restaurant located in the Tower Grove East neighborhood of old St. Louis City. From the drinks list to mouth-watering barbecue, it's evident that The Shaved Duck pays meticulous attention to every detail of the dining experience. The theme of the restaurant is "Barbecue, Folk and Soul" and the eclectic vibe and live music four nights a week appeal to a mixed demographic of patrons. Interestingly enough, I met a few Scots in the barbecue business including owners in Maine, Virginia and Missouri – Ally Nisbet at The Shaved Duck. The general story from these guys is that they had never tasted anything like American barbecue before coming to the states. Like an epiphany, once they experienced American barbecue, they dove into it and never looked back.

My favorite burnt ends in America are the tender, smoky and lightly sauced burnt ends at The Shaved Duck. The Walnut & Brown Sugar Encrusted Bacon is also a favorite. Cured in-house, smoked for six hours in their Ole Hickory Pits smoker and served with pears and bleu cheese, this thick bacon masterpiece is fit for any barbecue connoisseur. You also can't go wrong with the house-made sausage and thick mac 'n cheese.

Great service, an intimate atmosphere, thoughtful drinks list and unbelievable barbecue makes The Shaved Duck a great place to have a meal.

#20. B.T.'s Smokehouse

Sturbridge, Massachusetts

www.btsmokehouse.com

Established: 2009

Style: Chef-created traditional barbecue with a slight Texas accent.

Wood: Apple, hickory and cherry.

What to try: Brisket Reuben, buffalo wings and mustard sauce.

What to avoid: Beans.

I wasn't sure what to expect when I arrived at B.T.'s Smokehouse in the small, South-Central Massachusetts town of Sturbridge. B.T.'s had received its fair share of positive local press, but local barbecue press in the Northeast is not always to be trusted. I arrived in the evening thinking "It's late so things have probably been sitting for a few hours." I was happy to say my Northeastern media bias and readymade excuses for poor barbecue were completely out of line. B.T. delivered.

Chef-Owner Brian Treitman decided it was time to leave fine dining and enter the barbecue world in, of course, rural Massachusetts. B.T.'s started as a trailer catering festivals and events. Today, you will likely find a 20-30 person line at 11AM with 900 people finding smoked satisfaction each day in the 40 seat restaurant. If you make great barbecue, they will come.

Highlights include the brisket, Brisket-Reuben sandwich, mustard sauce and wings.

#21. Gates Bar-B-Q

Kansas City, Missouri
www.gatesbbq.com
Established: 1946
Style: Old Kansas City classic. Know what you want.
Wood: Hickory.
What to try: Sauce, burnt ends, sauce, ham, more sauce.
What to avoid: Not getting enough sauce.

If a restaurant made their name and stakes their reputation on a sauce, there will be plenty of people who don't like it. I understand this. For all of the other sauce-slathering places out there that I visited and didn't care for because I didn't love the sauce, plenty of people will feel the same way about Gates. I however, love Gates' black pepper-heavy, tomato-based sauce. For me, this is what barbecue sauce is all about.

While I say it's all about the sauce, the burnt ends at Gates are excellent and the ham is a nice break from the normal barbecue fare. The fries are nothing special, but they make a great vehicle for the sauce.

With the two Kansas City restaurants ahead of it being relative newcomers on the barbecue scene, Kansas City needed an old guard restaurant in the Top 25. When it comes to the old and established joints, Kansas City residents are generally split between Arthur Bryant's and Gates. I respect anyone who prefers Bryant's, but I'm a Gates guy.

#22. J.R.'s Rhodehouse BBQ Pit

Piedmont, South Dakota

www.jrsbbqpit.com

Established: 2013

Style: Texas.

Wood: Oak, sometimes pecan.

What to try: Burnt ends, turkey, brisket, mac 'n cheese.

What to avoid: All sides but the mac 'n cheese. Just double or
triple down here.

There were many places in America where I asked myself "Why am I looking for barbecue here?" South Dakota was one of those places. J.R.'s Rhodehouse BBQ Pit, however, made the many hours of driving across the Dakotas worthwhile. A few of my favorite restaurants are relatively undiscovered restaurants in places like Austin or Memphis, but J.R.'s is the first to come way out of left field. It is absolutely incredible, though.

J.R.'s Rhodehouse became homeless a few months before my visit when an arson fire damaged the restaurant. They moved into the local VFW temporarily and now cater out of J.R.'s home. Caterers were not considered for this list, but J.R.'s serves individual plates on the weekends and they were too good for me to leave off.

The brisket was terrific and probably what J.R. is most proud of, but the turkey and burnt ends were even better. The brisket is simple, well-executed, salt and pepper-rubbed, foil-wrapped and oak-smoked. The burnt ends were rich, plump and tender with tremendous amounts of char. The turkey was moist and perfectly smoked. The two-cheese mac 'n cheese with bacon and a little bit of hot sauce is smoked for about 20 minutes and spot on. This is what mac 'n cheese at a barbecue restaurant should be. I had hundreds of mac 'n cheeses around the country before trying this. One bite and I knew it was the best I had ever had.

One purpose of this project was to give the small town guys in places like Piedmont the opportunity to compete against the big boys in barbecue. More often than not they don't compare well, but J.R.'s Rhodehouse shows that great barbecue can be found in small towns outside barbecue country. I ate a lot of bad barbecue in places like Nebraska, New Mexico and Delaware to find it, but J.R.'s made all of that worthwhile.

#23. Smoque BBQ

Chicago, Illinois

www.smoquebbq.com

Established: 2006

Style: Busy neighborhood spot creating its own style and
    uninhibited by local expectations.

Wood: Apple, oak.

What to try: Brisket, mac 'n cheese, pecan bread pudding.

What to avoid: The line…give yourself time.

Smoque BBQ is the most heralded and recognized barbecue restaurant in Chicago. I had the pleasure of meeting Owner Barry Sorkin to learn about Smoque, swap barbecue stories and try a little top notch 'que.

Everyone in Chicago talks about the brisket at Smoque and it's the best I found in town. I also thoroughly enjoyed the mac 'n cheese and pecan bread pudding - these happen to be the three things Barry recommends as well.

Below is part of the conversation we had.

Me: What got you into barbecue?

Barry: I grew up in a northern suburb of Chicago where there wasn't any real BBQ. We had some rib places that put BBQ sauce on a slab, but it was a pretty far cry from low-and-slow smoked BBQ. I didn't know any better.

When I was in high school, I was working at a local hardware store and one day I remember smelling something incredible from across the room. I followed it into the break room where a bunch of my co-workers were eating. They had made the trip to Evanston to pick up Hecky's BBQ. I had never heard of it, but more importantly, I had never smelled anything that good. Sadly, all that was left were scraps, but I ate the scraps and instantly fell in love. A few years later, I started playing around in the backyard and learning to smoke stuff myself.

In a notoriously difficult industry, how has Smoque thrived and received such a great reputation?

You know, we've just always focused on putting out good BBQ and we let everything else fall into place. We were very lucky to get a lot of great press early on and throughout the first few years. So we had lots of people coming in to give us a try. We knew that all we had to do was make sure they got a great experience and they would be back and they'd bring friends.

How would you describe Chicago barbecue?

Chicago has become an interesting BBQ town. Historically, Chicago BBQ has been ribs, rib tips, and hot links. But today, we have a huge BBQ scene that pays homage to all of the great BBQ cities around the country. The nice thing about being in a city that doesn't have terribly deep BBQ roots is that we can draw on influences from anywhere without feeling like we're abandoning our heritage. In other words, native Chicagoans are open to all kinds of BBQ because most of us didn't grow up with a particular style as part of our culture. Right now, we've got some of the city's best culinary talent interpreting some of the country's best BBQ styles. It's very exciting.

How would you describe your barbecue?

We were one of the early places to try to bring together our favorite styles from around the country together in one place. But it was never our intention to mimic anything. We wanted to do our version of everything. So while our brisket, for example, is definitely Texas (specifically Austin) style, it is somewhat different from anything I've had out there.

#24. Heirloom Market BBQ

Atlanta, Georgia
www.heirloommarketbbq.com
Established: 2010
Style: Korean-American blend uniquely their own.
Wood: Hickory and oak.
What to try: Brunswick stew, chips, pulled pork.
What to avoid: I wasn't disappointed with anything.

Heirloom Market is my favorite barbecue spot in the Atlanta area and I bet it's unlike anything you have ever had. Korean barbecue is big business and wonderful in its own right, but outside the scope of this project. Heirloom, however, makes top notch American barbecue with twists of Korean flavor. Chefs and Owners Cody and Jiyeon mirrored this approach with their other restaurant, Sobban - Korean with a Southern twist.

Cody and Jiyeon are one of the most interesting couples in barbecue. Careers in fine dining brought them together, but their backgrounds couldn't be more different. Cody grew up with American barbecue in Southeast Texas while Jiyeon was a Korean pop star – I'm not kidding. The miso-injected brisket and kimchi mayo exemplify this union at Heirloom Market.

Heirloom is a tiny storefront with an outdoor patio tucked into an odd location between a highway and the old Riverbend Apartments of *Catch Me If You Can* fame. The bright red sign makes it difficult to miss as you drive by.

The Brunswick stew is the item that stood out the most and it's one of the best you will ever taste. The thick, sweet chips were also inexplicably good. The pulled pork was my favorite of the meats, but the Korean pork is worth trying simply because it is out of the ordinary. The brisket, turkey, wings, beans, greens and pork ribs were well done and I won't steer you away from any of those options.

#25. City Butcher and Barbecue *

Springfield, Missouri

www.citybutchersgf.com

Established: 2014

Style: Texas.

Wood: White oak.

What to try: Burnt ends, sausages, brisket.

What to avoid: Pork and sides aren't bad, but the burnt ends and
sausage are amazing.

* City Butcher and Barbecue is the one restaurant in the Top 100
that I did not visit as part of my 365 barbecue restaurant tour. My
visit happened after. I was so impressed, however, that I wanted
to include them in this book – and in the Top 25.

Owners Jeremy Smith and Cody Smith, despite not being related,
share much more in common than a last name. Each grew up just
outside Springfield (Nixa and Rogersville). Both went to Le
Cordon Bleu – Jeremy in Arizona and Cody in Texas. While in
Texas to learn fine dining in the classroom, Cody fell in love with
Texas-style barbecue outside the classroom. Cody wasn't new to
barbecue. He had, in fact, managed Rogersville's Skinner's Ribs &
BBQ as a teenager. In Texas, however, things are different.

Upon returning to the Ozarks, both chefs paid their dues in fine
dining. They grew tired of it, though, and longed to prepare the
kind of food they actually eat themselves. Cody stepped out on

his own by creating Le Cochon Charcuterie and selling at the Farmer's Market of the Ozarks. Jeremy, during this time, was sous chef at a local restaurant.

City Butcher and Barbecue, as the name implies, is both a home for the charcuterie as well as a barbecue restaurant. Charcuterie offerings during my visit included duck pastrami, hot links, andouille, jagerwurst, beef tenderloin, duck ham and a couple of bacons.

Most Texas-style joints outside the Lone Star State fail miserably. City doesn't. The market-style, butcher paper, etc. are all fine, but it's the Texas-style food that impressed me.

Brisket is the top seller. During my visit, a woman was offered a bite of the brisket as she surveyed the menu. She immediately exclaimed, "Wow! I want that!" Three out of four visitors, many after a similar experience, order the brisket. Pork – either pulled pork or pork ribs – are the norm in this part of the country, so City is doing a bit of re-education as to what brisket really should be.

I tried a bit of everything and was not disappointed. The brisket (sourced from Creekstone Farms – also the provider to Franklin Barbecue) is excellent. City's brisket would do well in Texas, but it wouldn't be a revelation to Texans. Where City really excels is with the burnt ends and sausages. These are some of the best you will find anywhere. The sausages, as you might expect from a restaurant with a history in charcuterie, are fantastic. The burnt ends were not necessarily distinct in any particular way, but well-executed, tender, perfectly seasoned and an absolute delight.

My favorite of the three sides was the chunky potato salad made with baby Yukon and Red potatoes with cubed pickles. I won't blame you, however, if you skip the sides and stick with the meats.

The South

If the South is the crown of American cuisine, barbecue is the crown jewel. There are a lot of great places making barbecue in the South, but these are my favorites.

Bar-B-Cutie

Nashville, Tennessee
www.bar-b-cutie.com
Established: 1950
Style: Old, carhop inspired neighborhood joint.
Wood: Hickory.
What to try: Pork sandwich on cornbread pancakes with your
     favorite sauce.
What to avoid: Sandwich on anything but the cornbread
     pancakes.

I was unfamiliar with Bar-B-Cutie before my trip to Nashville, but readers ranging from the Mexican border to Ohio may be familiar with the brand as Bar-B-Cutie has franchised and grown in recent years. They even have three locations in Spain! A staple in Nashville neighborhoods for decades, Bar-B-Cutie was chosen Nashville's favorite barbecue by readers of The Tennessean six out of the last seven years. Four generations of the McFarland family have worked at Bar-B-Cutie, including three generations today.

I was impressed, and admittedly surprised, by the quality of barbecue in Nashville. Nashville will always be the barbecue step-child in Tennessee, but I found three Nashville restaurants worthy of the Top 100. The ribs at Bar-B-Cutie were average, but their signature pulled pork sandwich on cornbread pancakes was terrific. I fell in love with this sandwich. The cornbread pancakes might not be anything special on their own, but their light sweetness and griddle flavor complimented the classic pork, slaw and sauce combo so well. It's now my preferred bread or bun for a pork sandwich.

B.B. King's Blues Club

Memphis, Tennessee (3 locations)
www.bbkingclubs.com
Established: 1991
Style: Bar, live music venue.
Wood: Hickory.
What to try: A big plate of ribs.
What to avoid: Lunch. Go and enjoy a drink and live music with
   dinner.

My first stop in Memphis was B.B. King's Blues Club on Beale Street. I recognized B.B.'s as an iconic Memphis hotspot, but thought of it more as a bar and music venue than barbecue restaurant. I learned, however, that they actually do more food business than bar business and that the ribs are their number one seller...for good reason! The ribs were great. Marinated overnight in a special concoction of their barbecue sauce, fruit juices and spices, BB's braises their ribs and serves them either wet or dry.

Ribs are best accompanied by a cold beer and live music, so I stopped back in later that night to get the full B.B. King experience. It was 8PM or so, but I noticed that most people were having dinner and not simply drinking. I expected to hear nothing but good music at B.B. King's, but I was still surprised by the quality of the band. B.B.'s is a great place to share a meal, have some drinks and enjoy a fun evening with friends.

The Barbecue Exchange

Gordonsville, Virginia

www.bbqex.com

Established: 2011

Style: Trying to establish Virginia-style barbecue as salted, lightly spiced meat over green hickory.

Wood: Green hickory.

What to try: Pork, spicy slaw, peanut butter pie.

What to avoid: Brisket.

After a visit to Thomas Jefferson's Monticello, I ventured to the small town of Gordonsville, Virginia, where I met Owner/Chef Craig Hartman of The Barbecue Exchange. A friend was with me and, as we parked, I commented about there being a dog in the car to our right. Upon closer inspection, though, we found that someone had not left their dog in the car...but their goat! Welcome to rural Virginia!

Although it was 3PM, the restaurant was packed. The town of Gordonsville only has about a thousand residents, but The Barbecue Exchange typically has 800-1200 visitors a day. The friendly family next to us lived about 2 hours away, but visited regularly - four times, in fact, within the previous week. The Barbecue Exchange has become a rural Virginia barbecue destination.

It was a pleasure to talk barbecue with Chef Craig. His experience and training combine to create a restaurant experience uniquely his own. His fine dining background is exhibited by the 11 varieties of house-made pickles, pumpkin muffins and Double BLT featuring both barbecue pork belly and bacon.

I tried a little bit of everything including the house cured ham, pork belly, homemade sausage, ribs, brisket and a dozen sides. It may not be nearly as exciting as the other things on the menu, but I think it's hard to go wrong with the pulled pork. I'm always a sucker for something spicy and the spicy slaw was a little bit unusual and my favorite of the sides. Any meal at The Barbecue Exchange needs to end with something sweet and I enjoyed the light peanut butter pie.

Big Bob Gibson Bar-B-Q

Decatur, Alabama (2 locations)

www.bigbobgibson.com

Established: 1925

Style: Synonymous with Northern Alabama barbecue.

Wood: Hickory.

What to try: White chicken.

What to avoid: They are so proud of it that I would give it another
    shot, but I wasn't crazy about the brisket.

When we think of historic Texas barbecue restaurants, places like
Black's and Kreuz come to mind. Kansas City conjures images of
Gates and Arthur Bryant's. These places have storied traditions
that exemplify particular styles of barbecue. Big Bob Gibson's
actually *defines* a style of barbecue. A short drive from Huntsville,
Big Bob Gibson's is the number one reason people visit Decatur,
Alabama. Big Bob Gibson's competition team won *Memphis in*

May again in 2014 to become one of the most decorated teams in barbecue competition history.

Some of the most famous, historic and talked about barbecue restaurants didn't impress me, but I thought Big Bob Gibson's lived up to their reputation. The ribs, pork and turkey were all well done, but I was here for the chicken and it's what I suggest you try. The mayo-based, vinegary, tart, peppery version of a ranch dressing works some sort of white magic when it touches Big Bob Gibson's tender, smoky chicken. The whole chickens are dunked once in the white sauce, but I like to add more at the table.

Boone's Bar-B-Que Kitchen

Charlotte, North Carolina

www.boonesbarbque.com

Established: 2014

Style: Generations-old Carolina 'cue from a food truck.

Wood: Mainly hickory, but sometimes peach or cherry.

What to try: Brunswick stew, pork with Eastern Carolina or
        mustard sauce.

What to avoid: Brisket.

"Boone" Gibson was the man behind the barbecue at a couple of Charlotte's favorite barbecue restaurants, but found himself without a place to serve his 'cue a couple years ago. He teamed up with an old friend to open a food truck and they are doing things right.

Boone attended culinary school and has a varied career, but he really hit his niche with one particular barbecue-related dish. Locals, including his business partner Tom, called Boone asking for his Brunswick stew by the gallon. This led to packaging of sauces and spices and a business was born. When we think of food trucks, we envision tiny, cramped spaces, but Boone's has a spacious commissary where they do all of their prep and smoking. It's out of this space where Boone works his magic. The Brunswick stew is absolutely incredible, but it's also worth your time to try the pork with the tasty line of sauces.

Bubba's Barbecue

Eureka Springs, Arkansas
www.bubbasbarbecueeurekasprings.com
Established: 1979
Style: Memphis in an eclectic Eureka Springs diner.
Wood: Hardwood hammer handle factory scraps.
What to try: Saucy sandwich.
What to avoid: Anything else. Stick to the basics here.

In the late 1970's, Bubba visited a number of Memphis barbecue restaurants to study their brick pits before returning to Eureka Springs to build his own. Today, Bubba's Barbecue is the oldest sole proprietorship restaurant in Eureka Springs.

Eureka Springs is a quirky small town of aging hippies who occupy the Victorian homes that jut over the town's spiraling streets. Fitting in with the rest of this eclectic town, Bubba's Barbecue is full of character. Bubba is a self-proclaimed "Mexicophile" who makes a pilgrimage south of the border every year and the daily specials often showcase these Hispanic flavors.

Bubba recommends a first time visitor try the pulled pork sandwich or ribs. The ribs were meaty and cooked well, but I recommend the sandwich. Bubba is a firm believer that slaw belongs on a sandwich, but for customers who do not share this core belief, he serves slaw on the side and lets the customers top it themselves. Topped with slaw and slathered in sauce, I think you have yourself a heck-of-a sandwich at Bubba's.

Community Q BBQ

Decatur, Georgia

www.communityqbbq.com

Established: 2009

Style: Carolina influenced, but has its own style. Owner has
background in fine dining. Neighborhood feel.

Wood: Hickory.

What to try: Beans, mac 'n cheese, pulled pork.

What to avoid: Brisket.

Georgia may not have its own distinct style of barbecue, but, as
the unofficial capital of the South, Atlanta would be incomplete
without barbecue. A number of quality restaurants, including
Community Q, have popped up within the last ten years. The web
of connections between Atlanta owners reminded me of NFL
coaching trees – restaurants spun off from older restaurants but
you can still see their barbecue lineage in their practices and
products.

The regular menu at Community Q is simple and sticks to
traditional barbecue dishes, but the specials and salads are a bit

out of the barbecue norm. The mac 'n cheese at Community Q is similar to the mac 'n cheese at Grand Champion and Dave Poe's, but I had it first at Community Q. It's incredible. Try the mac 'n cheese, but you must also try the baked beans. Many restaurants (including some very highly regarded and famous barbecue restaurants) start with canned beans. Not Community Q. The consistency is thinner than the archetypical baked bean, but they are meaty and have the perfect blend of sweetness and spice. For a main, try the pulled pork.

Dead End BBQ

Knoxville, Tennessee
www.deadendbbq.com
Established: 2009
Style: Competitors with family recipes trying to carve out a place for Knoxville barbecue in an old barber shop turned convenience store.
Wood: Hickory and oak pellets.
What to try: Ribs, competition chicken, wings.
What to avoid: Beans.

Owner George Ewart's barbecue story began two generations ago. Even though grandma never had any idea her sauce would inspire the creation of Knoxville's favorite barbecue restaurant, George treasures the old index card with grandma's sauce recipe.

My meal at Dead End started out with the smoked sausage and smoked cheese platter. The pita, sausage, cheese, ground mustard and barbecue basting sauce all dusted with their rub put my appetite on the right track.

During my restaurant visits, my notes were normally descriptive and thorough. At Dead End, however, I simply wrote "Excellent" next to the wings, ribs and George's Competition Chicken. I was too busy enjoying the meal to write any more. I do not expect you to have any room for dessert at Dead End, but take a piece of the peanut butter cake home with you. Trust me.

(Note: if you think George looks a lot like David Brooks of the *New York Times*, you would be wrong. That actually was David Brooks, who I ran into in Annapolis wearing my Dead End BBQ shirt.)

Fat Boys Barbeque Ranch

Prattville, Alabama
www.fatboysbarbqueranch.com
Established: 1998
Style: Small town, Southern home cookin'.
Wood: Hickory.
What to try: Pork with honey and pineapple sauce, potato salad.
What to avoid: Chopped brisket.

North of Montgomery, Alabama, in the small town of Prattville, sits Fat Boys Bar-B-Que Ranch. Other than Dreamland, Fat Boys is the only restaurant I came across with a story of a divinely orchestrated opening. Similar to Dreamland, owners Danny and Gretchen said God gave them peace about opening the restaurant by saying "Trust me." God must have special favor on Alabama since both Dreamland and Fat Boys are located in the Yellowhammer state.

Everything but the pickles is made from scratch at Fat Boys and the meats are carefully tended over a hot bed of hickory. It's a small restaurant in a town where everyone knows everyone and I heard someone mention on his way out that he would be back sometime to oil the squeaky front door for Gretchen. While not much at Fat Boys is controversial, their ties to Auburn sports teams may cause a few eyes to roll in Mid-Alabama.

It's best to follow the KISS principle at Fat Boys. You can't go wrong with a pulled pork sandwich and potato salad. Their sauce is one of the sweetest I've had, and, while these are normally not my favorite, the honey pineapple sweetness worked with the pork.

Fox Bros. Bar-B-Q

Atlanta, Georgia

www.foxbrosbbq.com

Established: 2007

Style: Big and busy for good reason.

Wood: Hickory.

What to try: Pork and fried okra.

What to avoid: Falling trees.

Fox Bros. Bar-B-Q is Atlanta's most well-known barbecue restaurant. This inevitably leads some to say it's overrated, not what it used to be, or too commercial. I enjoyed it and found the food and atmosphere to equate to a quality barbecue experience. Bring some friends, share some plates of food and have some fun.

Every barbecue restaurant open for more than a year has experienced trying times, events or circumstances. For some it was a devastating fire. For others it was a personnel issue like a pitmaster leaving or change in management. For some it was an economic issue like the closing of the largest employer in the area. Occasionally it was receiving criticism from a respected local voice. For a few, like Fox Bros., it was natural disaster.

In 2012, a centenarian tree fell onto the restaurant forcing a brief closure and remodeling. The neighborhood jumped in to help and Fox Bros. came back better and stronger.

Full Service BBQ

Maryville, Tennessee
www.fullservicebbq.com
Established: 2007
Style: Beefed up parking lot serving incredible brisket.
Wood: Hickory and oak.
What to try: Brisket.
What to avoid: Pulled pork.

Full Service was a place that did not show up in my Knoxville research, but a local friend insisted I give it a shot. I was utterly surprised at what I found.

Full Service BBQ is my kind of place – laid back with American flags flying high over outdoor seating. Anthony DiFranco III opened shop a few years ago at what used to be a gas station. This isn't a convenience store kind of spot, though. This is a parking lot with only one of those tiny booths for a cashier. The lack of indoor space makes the Full Service experience more like a picnic than anything else. It has no bearing on the quality of the food, but I think it's cool that the fire burning in the smoker hasn't died in the last 5 years. Someone even stokes it on Christmas morning.

Full Service does a pretty darn good job with everything - including the ribs. *THE* thing to try, though, at Full Service is the brisket. It's one of the best you will find outside Texas.

Grand Champion BBQ

Roswell, Georgia (3 locations)

www.gcbbq.net

Established: 2011

Style: Fine dining meets competition meets suburban strip mall.

Wood: Hickory and oak.

What to try: Pork, mac 'n cheese.

What to avoid: Sausage.

As much as I've told this story, it would be uninteresting if I only told you the owners of Grand Champion BBQ have backgrounds in fine dining. This one has a slight twist, though. One of Grand Champion's founders is French. Not an American of French ancestry, but an actual Frenchman. That's not something often found in barbecue.

One might expect, from the restaurant's name, to see the walls lined with competition trophies. Co-owner Robert Owens (the non-French of the two) told me, however, that being Grand Champion means maintaining a certain level of excellence for the hundreds of judges who walk through the front door of the restaurant every day.

The ribs and mac 'n cheese were both delectable, but I think the pulled pork was the star of the show. A dash of the Carolina sauce took it over the top.

Henry's Smokehouse

Greenville, South Carolina (3 locations)

www.henryssmokehouse.com

Established: 1991

Style: The kind of place where your parents may have first met, the neighbor kid works or you go after a high school football game.

Wood: Hickory and oak.

What to try: Pork, fries, mustard sauce, sweet potatoes.

What to avoid: Not coming hungry.

I met Henry's Smokehouse manager, Tiger, who started with the restaurant 22 years ago washing dishes. I love seeing that sort of history, dedication and continuity in a barbecue restaurant staff.

The building was originally a general store when it was constructed in the 1920's or 1930's. 600 people a day are now fed in the small, 30 seat restaurant which has an old-school, eclectic, community feel. The barbecue community often supports veterans and the military. The weekend I visited, Henry's food truck partnered with a local masseuse to offer free barbecue and massages to vets.

Let's get down to the food. Tiger recommended a first time visitor try the chopped pork plate with sweet potatoes and banana pudding for dessert. That's exactly what I tried. The sweet potatoes were phenomenal, but the best bite at Henry's was a forkful of pork and fries dipped in the terrific spicy mustard sauce. The flavor of the pork, crispiness of the fries and bite of the spicy mustard all added up to barbecue nirvana. Even when I slowed down on the pork, fries and sweet potatoes, somehow my tongue took control of my hand and kept feeding bites of the white bread smothered in the spicy mustard sauce into my mouth.

Lexington Barbecue

Lexington, North Carolina

www.lexbbq.com

Established: 1962

Style: Heard of Lexington-style BBQ? Well…

Wood: Oak and hickory.

What to try: Chopped plate or tray.

What to avoid: Asking for unsweetened tea.

Lexington Barbecue is one of the iconic porkhouses in America. When I discussed travel plans through North Carolina or reminisced about my visits with restaurant owners around the country, Lexington Barbecue almost always entered the conversation. It's a must visit for any barbecue fan.

Along my travels, I met the North Carolina-based bloggers from www.barbecuebros.co. They talk about Lexington as if there is no place better on the face of the earth. It's the standard by which all Carolina barbecue is judged. Carolinians' favorite restaurants largely depend on regional preferences, but Lexington has its apologists all across the state. It is not everyone's favorite style, as it isn't mine, but it's hard to say anything bad about it. I tried many of the historic barbecue houses along the Highway 52 and I-85 corridor and Lexington Barbecue was my favorite.

Things are simple at Lexington. Hickory and oak coals slow-smoke pork shoulders and the slaw is revered as other-worldly by Lexington faithful. The sauce has some tomato, but is predominantly vinegar. The pork, slaw and sauce is considered the core of the experience and everything else at Lexington Barbecue is proudly called "secondary."

Martin's Bar-B-Que Joint

Nolensville, Tennessee (4 locations)

www.martinsbbqjoint.com

Established: 2006

Style: Old meets new. Respecting traditions, but using them in creative ways.

Wood: Hickory.

What to try: Patrick Martin says everyone should be judged by their pork sandwich.

What to avoid: Ribs.

Martin's Bar-B-Que Joint didn't take long to become one of Nashville's favorites. The Nolensville store opened in 2006, and, in less than ten years, Martin's has grown to four locations. Pat Martin has been making barbecue for 20 years and he took the restaurant plunge eight years ago by using his house as collateral for the first location. Pat considers himself a traditionalist and not a competition guy. Martin's tries to do things the right way which includes using large cuts of meat, not having a freezer or microwave in the kitchen and providing extensive training for the pitmasters who become part owners of each location.

Pat recommends the pork sandwich since he believes this is how barbecue restaurants should be judged. I tried the pork sandwich, wings in White Alabama Sauce, house-made sausage, ribs, brisket and "Redneck Taco" (cornbread pancake topped with meat, slaw and sauce - basically an open faced sandwich). You will not be disappointed if you take Pat's challenge of judging Martin's by the pork sandwich, but my favorites were the Redneck Taco and house-made sausage.

Maurice's Piggie Park BBQ

Columbia, South Carolina (14 locations)
www.piggiepark.com
Established: 1939
Style: South Carolina through and through.
Wood: Oak and hickory.
What to try: Hash 'n rice, pork, ribs, wings, sauces.
What to avoid: The brisket was above average for the Southeast, but stick to the pork.

Many of South Carolina's famous barbecue restaurants are in small towns scattered across the state, but perhaps the Palmetto State's most famous barbecue brand is Maurice's Piggie Park. At one time, Maurice's Yellow Gold was the best-selling barbecue sauce in America - incredible since it's a mustard-based sauce. Today Maurice's has 14 restaurants in Central South Carolina.

As soon as I mentioned the Piggie Park to anyone in the Carolinas, the conversation steered away from barbecue and towards politics. Maurice Bessinger, founder of the Piggie Park, was a divisive character who stepped beyond barbecue to issues of race, history and politics. He passed away shortly before my visit and the younger generation has done their best to honor their father, but move on from his controversial spotlight.

All of that aside, I enjoyed my meal at the Piggie Park. The Yellow Gold is distinctive and certainly the place to start at Maurice's, but I found the hot pepper sauce to even be a notch better. Maurice's probably has the best one-two sauce punch anywhere in the country.

A first time visitor should try what Maurice's is known for: sauced chopped pork with hash 'n rice on the side. South Carolina barbecue is generally described by the iconic mustard sauce, but hash 'n rice is another distinctive South Carolina barbecue dish. There are a range of hash styles, but a yellowish/gray, peppery, vinegary, tightly minced, thick stew served over white rice is most common. It often doesn't look appealing, but after a bite, that doesn't seem to matter.

Some people will love or hate the Piggie Park solely because of its style of barbecue. I think it's a solid representation of South Carolina barbecue and a great place to get a meal.

Memphis Barbecue Co.

Horn Lake, Mississippi (3 locations)
www.memphisbbqco.com
Established: 2011
Style: As the name might suggest…
Wood: Pecan.
What to try: Pulled pork, ribs, crème brulee.
What to avoid: If Memphis is in the name, skip the beef.

Memphis Barbecue Co. has only been in business a couple years, but they are growing quickly. I sat down with two-time *Memphis in May* Grand Champion, Melissa Cookston who teamed up with fellow Grand Champion, John David Wheeler to open the Memphis Barbecue Co.

Some customers will appreciate this and some will not, but Memphis Barbecue Co. feels more like a corporate restaurant than hole-in-the-wall barbecue joint. I'll attribute this to the large box of a building, slick marketing and robust menu. This does not mean, however, that every dish is not given individual attention. The menu has a wide scope and I enjoyed sampling everything from cheese fritters to bacon wrapped shrimp (with house cured bacon…delicious!) to crème brulee. I was told the wet baby back ribs are the signature dish, but I was most pleased with the pulled pork. Try both and let me know which you enjoy more.

Midwood Smokehouse

Charlotte, North Carolina
www.midwoodsmokehouse.com
Established: 2011
Style: Mix of Eastern and Western Carolina…and a little Texas.
Wood: Hickory.
What to try: Brisket.
What to avoid: The temptation to dismiss any brisket in the
      Carolinas.

While Kansas City and Memphis barbecue are centered in major metropolitan areas, Texas and Carolina barbecue are spread across smaller towns and rural areas. Even though towns like Lexington and Ayden are more famous for barbecue than Charlotte or Raleigh, barbecue is in the DNA of the whole state. The small-town joints maintain their old-school barbecue character while many of the restaurants that have popped up over the last decade in Charlotte or Raleigh have a more polished feel. Midwood Smokehouse, opened by Charlotte restaurateur Frank Scibelli, is one of those places. The full bar, modern interior, slick website and focus on barbecue items outside the traditional pork and slaw make for a different barbecue experience than you find at a traditional North Carolina barbecue joint.

It's trendy for barbecue restaurants east of the Mississippi to be proud of their brisket, but only a handful of these restaurants are genuinely able to back it up. Midwood is one of the few. Midwood's staff spent time studying, learning and eating in Texas to learn from the masters and their tasty brisket is the evidence.

Everything I had was well-executed. The ribs were good enough to be the recommended item at most restaurants, but it wasn't the star at Midwood. The brisket is the best bite and Midwood's brisket is the best beef you will find in the Carolinas.

Mike & Jeff's BBQ

Greenville, South Carolina

www.mikeandjeffsbbq.com

Established: 1996

Style: Tiny South Carolina shack.

Wood: Hickory, oak and pecan.

What to try: Pulled chicken, mustard sauce, sweet potatoes.

What to avoid: Ribs, potato salad, beans.

Mike & Jeff's isn't the kind of place that will dazzle you with a website, garner media attention or create buzz within the foie gras-eating foodie community. It's a shack. Some might call it a dump.

My experience with Mike & Jeff's was an interesting one. I first passed through Greenville, South Carolina, one Sunday afternoon and visited a couple of other spots around town. One restaurant was quite bad, but I was impressed with Henry's Smokehouse. Having found a spot worthy of the Top 100, I was pleased with my work in Greenville. As I shared my project with some locals, the group's biggest barbecue fan insisted I visit Mike & Jeff's. I came across Mike & Jeff's in my research, but knew they were closed on Sundays and Mondays – the two days I would be in town. He was incredibly disappointed I wouldn't experience what he considered the best barbecue in his beloved town. I promised to try to make it back to Greenville.

A few months later, I made it back with Mike & Jeff's being my only barbecue stop in town. I was not disappointed. Mike & Jeff's is exactly what comes to mind when you think of a hole-in-the-wall. Everything is old. Not vintage beer and gas company tin signs, but just average, old stuff like you might find at your grandparent's home in the 1990's.

Pork is Mike & Jeff's best seller, but I found it to be good, not great. The redeeming factor for the pork, however, was the fantastic golden mustard sauce. I wouldn't mind a plate of pork with the golden sauce, but the chicken was the protein that wowed me. The shredded chicken was tender, smoky, lightly sauced and absolutely perfect. The ribs were disappointing and the sides, with one exception, were average. The sweet potatoes, the exception, were amazing.

This is another reason people have such a range of experiences with barbecue restaurants. Had I visited Mike & Jeff's for a plate of ribs and beans, the experience would have been below average. Judged on the chicken, golden sauce and sweet potatoes alone, it would be a Top 25 place. Some restaurants are solid across the board while others shine with a couple of items but do not impress with others. Mike & Jeff's was one of those places for me, but the chicken, golden sauce and sweet potatoes were good enough to outweigh a few misses.

Momma's Mustard, Pickles & BBQ

Louisville, Kentucky (2 locations)

www.mommasbbq.com

Established: 2012

Style: Kansas City barbecue in a historic home-turned-bar.

Wood: Hickory.

What to try: Wings, beef rib, pickles.

What to avoid: Most of the rest of the barbecue around Louisville.

I did not know of Louisville's bourgeoning food scene until my most recent visit. The quality of restaurants in most cities has improved with the rise of foodie culture, food television and a renewed resistance to processed foods. Louisville is unique, I was told, in that much of the freshest food in America is found here because of the massive UPS hub at Louisville's airport. One might order lobster or sushi at a beachside restaurant and unknowingly consume seafood that passed through Louisville. Everything the world eats is just a plane ride away for Louisville restaurants.

Momma's Mustard, Pickles & BBQ was opened by Kansas City native Chad Cooley after he found the barbecue scene in Louisville to leave something to be desired. As the name implies, this isn't your normal barbecue joint. First, it's in a house turned restaurant/basement bar/beer garden. The mustard and pickles were good, but still mustard and pickles. The two must-try items at Momma's are the wings and beef ribs. The smoked, rubbed, flash-fried wings are crispy, addictive and delicious. I've found beef ribs along my journey to be hit or miss: some are good, but most disappoint. Momma's beef ribs do not disappoint.

Momma's also has a unique giving program called 2% for Louisville. A 1% surcharge is added to each customer's bill which is then matched by Momma's. Customer's vote for one of six local organizations (such as the Special Olympics of Kentucky) and the total money raised by the 2% for Louisville program is divided among the six charities based on the total votes. It's a great program that demonstrates what it means for a restaurant to be a caring, committed and invested member of a community.

Moonlite Bar-B-Q Inn

Owensboro, Kentucky

www.moonlite.com

Established: Early 50's. Became what it is today after being bought by Bosley family in 1963.

Style: Defines Owensboro barbecue.

Wood: Hickory.

What to try: Mutton, desserts.

What to avoid: Country sides.

Memphis, the Carolinas, Texas and Kansas City all consider themselves the center of the barbecue world, but they aren't the only ones. Owensboro, Kentucky, promotes itself as such, but most casual barbecue fans have never heard of it. Owensboro's claim to barbecue fame is mutton. More like Big Bob Gibson and Northern Alabama-style barbecue than any single restaurant in the big four barbecue regions, Moonlite Bar-B-Q Inn defines its style of barbecue.

Moonlite is an experience unlike any other. The scope of the restaurant is astounding. They have a massive shipping center, the biggest pits I have ever seen and the restaurant seats 325 customers. A visit is like a step back in time as very little seems to have changed in a generation or two at Moonlite.

So what about the food? Mutton isn't my favorite, but barbecue fans should try it. Most people visit Moonlite for the buffet, which I normally do not enjoy. The old-fashioned sides, like butter beans, also are not my favorites. A trip to Moonlite isn't complete without a trip through their selection of delicious desserts. With these, I'm fully on board.

As you can tell, I'm not crazy about the food at Moonlite – except for the desserts. Moonlite is so unique, though, I wanted to include it. A visit to experience this slice of barbecue culture, history and flavor is a must for any barbecue fan.

Rendezvous

Memphis, Tennessee
www.hogsfly.com
Established: 1948
Style: Barbecue museum and face of Memphis barbecue.
Wood: Charcoal.
What to try: Ribs, cheese and sausage plate, slaw.
What to avoid: Bringing your own barbecue bias. Just enjoy
      Rendezvous for what it is.

Charlie Vergos' Rendezvous may be the most famous barbecue restaurant in the world. Thousands of locals and visitors enjoy the charcoal-broiled pork ribs each week in the back-alley-basement-of-wonders that is The Vous. I sat down with Owner John Vergos to learn about this barbecue institution.

The Vous was the first restaurant to sell ribs at any notable scale. When they started in 1948, ribs were a discarded meat sold for 10 cents a pound. Ribs are, of course, synonymous with barbecue today and Rendezvous was the driving force behind this. John doesn't care for the term "dry rubbed ribs", but it all started at Rendezvous.

Despite being the face of Memphis barbecue and owning a distinct place in barbecue lore, Rendezvous does their ribs differently. First, they use charcoal instead of wood and direct heat rather than indirect heat which results in a much shorter cook time. A small minority of barbecue restaurants, including Rendezvous, leave the rack-long, tough membrane on their ribs because, they argue, it helps hold the moisture of the meat. Rendezvous' iconic slaw is a 1915-ish recipe from John's grandfather's hot dog stand. Like the ribs, the strong mustard and vinegar slaw isn't going to please everyone, but it's just the way it's always been done at Rendezvous. I actually love it.

The experience at Rendezvous is one of the best in barbecue. Much of America's culture passed through the restaurant and the walls reflect much of this today. One of my favorite stories from Rendezvous came from the Rolling Stones' first US tour in 1964. John's dad threw them out for their poor behavior.

Some barbecue folks love Rendezvous' style of barbecue and consider it the gold standard. Others say its day has passed. I'm in the middle. I appreciate what they do. I respect their devotion to their style, tastes, methods and history. The style isn't my favorite, but the food is good. The atmosphere is amazing and I think it's an essential stamp in any barbecue passport. Rendezvous isn't like Moonlite, which I recommend visiting once. Even though it isn't my very favorite style, Rendezvous will be in my regular Memphis rotation and I look forward to visiting again the next time I'm in town.

Saw's BBQ

Homewood, Alabama

www.sawsbbq.com

Established: 2009

Style: North Carolina/Southern shack.

Wood: Green hickory.

What to try: Ribs.

What to avoid: A tight schedule. There will likely be a line.

I talked to a number of locals during my visit to Birmingham and Saw's BBQ was, without a doubt, the most recommended barbecue restaurant in the area. The crowded, little space was bustling during my visit and I happened to run into George Vlahakis of the Barbecued Adventures blog during my visit.

Many of my favorite barbecue restaurants have owners or chefs with backgrounds in fine dining. Mike Wilson also took this path after completing culinary school and working at Dean & DeLuca. There is just something about barbecue that draws people back and brings them home to the smells, flavors and camaraderie of youth and family.

The ribs at Saw's are probably the thing to try although they will not please every palate. They are sauced, have an excellent level of spice and are quite charred. Dry-rub devotees, the spice-intolerant or those who think char distorts the flavors of the meat will not find these to be their favorite. For those people, I recommend trying the pulled chicken sandwich with white barbecue sauce. Be sure to ask for extra sauce, though, as I found myself unable to get enough of it.

Smoke Ring

Atlanta, Georgia

www.smokeringatlanta.com

Established: 2013

Style: Rustic yet modern; chef-owned.

Wood: Hickory and apple.

What to try: Pork, fried green tomato, corn on the cob.

What to avoid: Brisket.

Jordan and Erin Wakefield found a home. The couple was involved in a variety of restaurants before Smoke Ring, but this is not just another stop on the road. It's theirs. The menu, aesthetics, and culture are all their own.

Not far from downtown Atlanta, Smoke Ring anchors a redeveloping neighborhood. The open, beautiful space features rich earth tones and thoughtful finishes. The table I sat at was built into an antique revolving door frame from a New York hotel.

Smoke Ring offers the usual barbecue fares in its robust menu. The chef in Jordan is always thinking, tinkering and experimenting and you might find a special of the day like smoked octopus, quail or venison. Hickory wood is predominantly used and the antibiotic and hormone-free meats all come from organic farms. Well, maybe not the octopi.

The fried green tomato with goat cheese, chow-chow and red pepper jam is not to be missed. The chipotle corn on the cob with cotija cheese was excellent and not something you often see. I could enjoy a great meal at Smoke Ring by just eating the sides and appetizers, but, come on, we're talking barbecue. My favorite of the meats was the pulled pork. You can pair it with your choice of bourbon chipotle, white, house or mustard sauces if you like or just enjoy the meat on its own.

Smoke Ring is more similar to The Granary, Chicago q, SMOKE and a number of urban, chef-run barbecue restaurants than the rustic, country restaurant we typically associate with barbecue. I would certainly hate to lose the old-school barbecue joints, but I think there is space for nicer restaurants within barbecue. I bet it will not take more than a few bites for you to agree.

Smokin' Okies

Oklahoma City, Oklahoma

www.thesmokinokies.com

Established: 2010

Style: Mobile food truck.

Wood: Hickory and oak pellets.

What to try: SOB, pork and pineapple stew.

What to avoid: Coming late. When it's gone, it's gone.

It's difficult to do barbecue well out of a food truck, but Smokin' Okies is doing just that. Smokin' Okies' ribs are blue ribbon winners and the brisket chili was crowned state champion, but there were two items I enjoyed more. First, let me introduce you to the SOB.

The Smokin' Okies Burrito is a generous portion of pork, creamy slaw and their fresh barbecue sauce rolled in a flour tortilla and grilled with a touch of butter. It's more or less the wrap version of a Memphis-style pulled pork sandwich, but I may like the wrap more than the sandwich. The crispy, warm, buttery tortilla compliments the other components and plays a less prominent role in each bite than a bun. This allows one to fully experience the blended magic that is pork, barbecue sauce and slaw.

Second, I thought the smoked pork and pineapple stew was terrific. Pork and pineapple may not be an old-school barbecue combination, but we know it's good. Canadian bacon and pineapple works on pizza. Fruity barbecue sauces, including those featuring pineapple, have grown in popularity the last few years and are often paired with pork. It's sweet, but a slightly different kind of sweet. The potato casserole was an excellent side and I think Smokin' Okies is one food truck worth chasing.

Smokin Pig: The Bar-B-Q Joint

Pooler, Georgia (2 locations)
www.smokinpigbbqjoint.com
Established: 2007
Style: Southern. Nothin' fancy, but good.
Wood: Oak.
What to try: Pulled pork with vinegar sauce or mustard sauce.
What to avoid: Any other meat.

A friend in the Savannah area said Smokin Pig was THE place to go for good barbecue. I took his recommendation, connected with owner Kevin Fabre and was glad I did.

The mild sauce dates back four generations, but Smokin Pig is a relatively recent hobby run wild. Savannah has a reputation for

169

good food, but one local claimed it to be overrated with more tourist traps than anything else. Whether or not this is true, both locations of Smokin Pig are away from Downtown Savannah and pull a predominantly local crowd. For a barbecue restaurant, that's always a good sign.

Without a doubt, the thing to get at Smokin Pig is the dry-rubbed, hand-pulled, lean, smoky pulled pork. Add a little bit of the spicy vinegar sauce and you have yourself a bite that will make you squeal with delight. If vinegar isn't your thing, the spicy mustard sauce is also quite good. I recommend the beans and mac 'n cheese for sides.

Sweet Rack Rib Shack

Tallahassee, Florida/Troy, Alabama
www.sweetrackribshack.com
Established: 2012/2015
Style: The Dickens blend.
Wood: Cherry.
What to try: Wings, brisket.
What to avoid: Skipping dessert.

The cynical observer might write off Sweet Rack Rib Shack as simply a college town restaurant with girls in tank tops. Upon further investigation (and a few bites!), it is clear there is much more to Sweet Rack than meets the eye. Sweet Rack is owned by a couple - Chris and Amanda Dickens. During my visit, Sweet Rack was in Tallahassee, Florida. After my visit and the birth of the Dickens' first child, they moved to Troy, Alabama, to be near family. Rather than travel or be an absentee owner, they closed the Tallahassee store and reopened, under the exact same name, menu, etc. in Troy.

Chris's background in fine dining includes training at the Culinary Institute of America and baking instruction from Le Cordon Bleu Paris. He assumed this knowledge would easily translate to top quality barbecue so he and Amanda bought the cheapest smoker they could find at Wal-Mart and entered a competition. They ended up in last place in every category except pork. Rather than walk away in defeat, Chris used this as motivation. Soon they were winning competitions and absolutely killing any competition with a dessert section.

Sweet Rack Rib Shack was born out of this success and quickly became a Tallahassee favorite. The brisket and wings are terrific, but the brisket is only served on Fridays. If you try the pork, give the mustard sauce a chance even if it isn't normally your favorite kind of sauce. The Bourbon Pecan Cheesecake is top notch – one of the best desserts I found in my travels.

The Pit

Raleigh, North Carolina
www.thepit-raleigh.com
Established: 2007
Style: Whole hog in a comfortable restaurant.
Wood: Oak and hickory blended with charcoal.
What to try: Whole hog, ribs, mac 'n cheese.
What to avoid: Brisket.

Located in an old, brick-walled, former packing plant, The Pit helped revitalize a neighborhood near downtown Raleigh. While The Pit offers a full service restaurant experience with quality drinks and desserts, their focus is remaining true to the old, North Carolina smoking traditions. They are not cooking in a hole in the ground, but the principles, woods and techniques remain the same. As owner Greg Hatem told me, The Pit improves barbecue by going backwards rather than forwards.

The thing to try at The Pit, of course, is the chopped whole hog. It's excellent. I was also impressed with both the baby back and spare ribs. The mac 'n cheese was my favorite side, but The Pit also takes great pride in its heirloom collards. It has a different feel than the traditional North Carolina joint, but I liked it. I'll be back the next time I'm in Raleigh.

Ubons Barbeque of Yazoo

Yazoo City, Mississippi

www.ubons.net

Established: 2003

Style: Southern home cookin' with competition and Memphis
       inspired food.

Wood: Hickory, occasionally pecan.

What to try: Ribs and pork.

What to avoid: Brisket.

The road between Little Rock and Jackson took me through the small town of Yazoo City, Mississippi. I stopped to visit Ubons Barbeque of Yazoo and hear a tale of family, food, barbecue competition, entrepreneurship and Bloody Mary Mix.

Ubons has immense pride in their 5th generation sauce (rightfully so, I might add), but it's the Bloody Mary Mix you might see in stores near you. The cocktails were such a hit on the competition barbecue circuit they decided to focus on drinks rather than the incredibly saturated barbecue sauce market.

The restaurant in Yazoo City is a fun, welcoming place and the barbecue is paid careful attention. "Daddy" spends most of his day around back manning the smoker and I was treated by everyone as if I had been a family friend my whole life. Reminding me of Gino's in Chicago, the walls are covered in notes, drawings and signatures by patrons. Competition trophies line the walls, but these are just a few of the hundreds won over many years.

The ribs are the thing to try at Ubons. I did not detect anything particularly unusual about them, but they were clearly prepared by an experienced hand. The rub seemed to have a hint of citrus, but other than that the rub is fairly mild and the ribs are served dry.

Whole Hog Café

Little Rock, Arkansas (13 locations)
www.wholehogcafe.com
Established: 2000
Style: Neighborhood competitors who made it big.
Wood: Pecan.
What to try: Ribs, potato salad.
What to avoid: Brisket.

It was a pleasure to meet "Sarge" from Whole Hog Cafe in Little Rock, Arkansas. Sarge is one of the most decorated competitors on the competition scene and has walked across the stage in Memphis around 15 times, placing in the top five in ribs four times. Not many people in the barbecue world can claim the same level of consistent excellence.

With 13 locations, Whole Hog Cafe has grown rapidly since it first opened on August 17, 2000. I stopped by the original brick and mortar location in Little Rock, Arkansas, and the 150 seat dining room was hopping - even at mid-afternoon in January.

My favorite item on the menu was the tangy, shorter, meaty ribs. The potato salad was also a highlight. With strong notes of sour cream and cream cheese, how could you go wrong?

Yellow Dog Eats

Gotha, Florida (2 locations)
www.yellowdogeats.com
Established: 1996
Style: Weird, beachy, sandwich shop.
Wood: Oak.
What to try: Any of the pork sandwiches.
What to avoid: The chips...but they may be unavoidable.

Yellow Dog Eats is my kind of place – eclectic, filled with locals and off-the-beaten-path (especially important in Orlando).

Yellow Dog Eats isn't strictly barbecue, but offers a variety of sandwiches - many of which include smoked pork. I sampled both "The Dog's 'Famous' Pulled Pork Sandwich" covered in a tangy, terrific gold sauce and the Hong Kong Fuey. The Hong Kong Fuey is a large pulled pork sandwich topped with toasted coconut, pickled jalapeños, chopped peanuts, pickled onions, peanut sauce, carrots and scallions. While I think the name is a bit misleading (perhaps Hanoi or Ho Chi Min would be more appropriate than Hong Kong), I thoroughly enjoyed it.

A small but workable bar is found inside; the patio serves as both a place to eat and a place to people watch. A couple at the next table had parrots on their shoulders and a group of teenage girls were having a great time inside the old VW bus that doubles as a booth. Yellow Dog Eats feels a world away from both the commercialism of Orlando and the stress of everyday life.

The biggest area for improvement that I see at YDE is with the sides. A bag of potato chips is something, but when compared to many of the great sides I've had along the way, they leave a bit to be desired. These great sandwiches deserve to be placed next to more than a bag of chips. Nevertheless, I enjoyed my visit to Yellow Dog Eats and recommend it to anyone visiting Orlando. You will not be disappointed with the sandwiches.

Midwest

The plains are windy, the people are friendly and the sauces are sticky in the Midwest. Kansas City still reigns supreme, but St. Louis and Chicago are quickly catching up.

17th Street BBQ

Murphysboro, Illinois (2 locations)
www.17thstreetbarbecue.com
Established: 1985
Style: Memphis meets bar at this big operation in a small town.
Wood: Apple.
What to try: Ribs, Lotta Bull sandwich.
What to avoid: Brisket by itself.

I did not simply meet a barbecue legend – I met "The Legend" at 17th Street BBQ in Murphysboro, Illinois. Mike Mills did not recall who dubbed him "The Legend", but he secured his place in barbecue history after winning *Memphis in May* a record three times. In addition to being involved in a few restaurants, Mike caters, teaches barbecue classes, competes and organizes the *Murphysboro Barbecue Cookoff*. I don't know when he sleeps.

Named Best Ribs in America by *Bon Appetit* and featured on the *Travel Channel, Good Morning America, Today Show, Food Network,* etc., these award-winning ribs are smoked for about six hours over a blend of apple and cherry woods in an Ole Hickory Pits smoker.

You have to try the ribs, but I also recommend the Lotta Bull sandwich. 17th Street BBQ adds grilled peppers and onions, horseradish-cheddar cheese, freshly cubed pickles, a fried egg and barbecue sauce to a bun-full of brisket for a heck of a sandwich.

Capitalist Pig

St. Louis, Missouri

www.capitalistpigbbq.com

Established: 2012

Style: 1937 art deco police station that is now an art gallery and one-of-a-kind barbecue joint.

Wood: Missouri white oak.

What to try: Ribs, potato salad, cornbread muffins and sampling of sauces.

What to avoid: Pulled pork.

I have not had the...opportunity...to enjoy a taxpayer funded meal in a Department of Corrections cafeteria, but I can say I've had a meal behind bars. An art deco jailhouse built as a WPA project in 1937 is home to an event space named Mad Art Gallery and the Capitalist Pig. Located just a stone's throw away from the Anheuser-Busch brewery in the Soulard neighborhood of St. Louis, visitors to the Capitalist Pig are first greeted by the aroma of grain and mash from the brewery. As if the unique atmosphere is not enough to distinguish the Capitalist Pig, Restaurateur Ron Buechele is passionate about partnering with local, socially responsible farmers to produce fresh food in a sustainable and socially conscious way. If someone in your group is vegetarian, you can still enjoy a meal at the Capitalist Pig as they offer vegetarian options of tofu and tempeh.

Hailing from a family composed of both Mediterranean and Central/South American blood, Ron brings these influences into his food. He listed brisket as his signature item, but I loved the ribs and burnt ends. Potato salads are rarely a favorite of mine, but the Capitalist Pig's made-to-order, fresh potato salad was unbelievable. The small, warm potato wedges covered in a dill, caper and tarragon sauce with red onion had just the right blend of spice and creaminess.

Capitalist Pig features seven unique, homemade sauces and sampling these was also a highlight. My favorite was the House sauce. Textured with multiple layers of flavor, the tamari and hoisin give it a slight Asian twist. I also thoroughly enjoyed the Blackberry Ancho and the Sweet and Smokey. The Vinegar sauce was first used in the kitchen until it was accidentally carried out to the floor. Customers started using it and liked it so it stayed. The Habanero Peach is surprisingly mild. The Jalapeno sauce had the most heat, but, if you have any spice tolerance whatsoever, it will not light you up. Finally, the homemade Sriracha closely matches the classic bottle of Sriracha we know, but in a fresh, preservative-less way.

Add these great sauces to quality meats, terrific sides and a unique atmosphere and you have an all-around great barbecue experience.

Chicago q

Chicago, Illinois
www.chicagoqrestaurant.com
Established: 2010
Style: Traditional barbecue in an urban, upscale atmosphere.
Wood: Apple and cherry.
What to try: Wings, grits, pulled pork, beans, mac 'n cheese.
What to avoid: This is one of the few barbecue restaurants to
        avoid if you haven't showered recently.

Although Chicago q is a very different experience from what most barbecue buffs enjoy at their favorite local joint, it tastefully combines barbecue tradition with the urban and modern.

Each meal at Chicago q starts with pickles and a complimentary basket of barbecue chips delivered to the table. I typically find barbecue chips overly salty and devoid of character, but Chicago q's were on point. It almost seemed odd to compliment the chips until I learned Chef/Partner Lee Ann Whippen is the only person with the recipe. She's found something that makes these stand above the rest and is keeping the secret to herself.

You'll need something to chase the chips and Chicago q has a collection of over 60 bourbons and whiskeys behind the bar. I tried the recently released Angel's Envy "q" bourbon. Although I'm not a regular bourbon drinker, I was surprised at how smooth I found the "q." If you have not found bourbon to be to your liking, perhaps "q" is a great place to start.

Appetizers range from a BBq flight (samples of brisket, pork and chicken) to crab cakes and fried green tomatoes. I highly recommend trying the Smoked Dry-Rub Wings, which are some of the best wings I've ever had.

Main course options include specialty items such as limited competition pork ribs and Kobe beef ribs. I enjoyed the pulled pork the most - especially when paired with the terrific house vinegar sauce.

I found the Kobe Brisket Baked Beans and Bruleed Macaroni and Cheese to be excellent and appreciated the variety of salad options as well.

Outstanding food and drink. Fantastic atmosphere. Chicago q is a terrific spot for 'cue.

Eli's Barbeque

Cincinnati, Ohio

www.elisbarbeque.com

Established: 2011

Style: Funky, Ohio conglomeration.

Wood: Hickory.

What to try: Pulled pork sandwich with slaw.

What to avoid: Saying you are from Texas, KC, Memphis, the
　　　　Carolinas, the South, etc.

Eli's Barbeque is my choice for the Cincinnati area. It's a bit off of
the beaten path, but worth the trip. Eli's has a unique feel that
starts with a classic barbecue joint, throws in a side of retro and a
dash of eclectic. I like it.

The pulled pork sandwich with slaw on top, ribs and jalapeño
cheese grits, were all enjoyable. While I often limit how much I eat
at each restaurant, I cleaned my plate at Eli's.

Hendricks BBQ

St. Charles, Missouri

www.hendricksbbq.com

Established: 2012

Style: Full-service, professionally-run bar and restaurant.

Wood: Apple and cherry.

What to try: Ribs, pastrami or burger.

What to avoid: Not having a drink.

An old Municipal Water Works building featuring an artfully decorated interior, eye-catching bar, partially open kitchen and attentive staff make Hendricks a perfect setting for a great plate of barbecue.

Despite not being a regular whiskey drinker, I enjoyed the Ginger Manhattan from the beguiling cocktail list. Hendricks has one of Missouri's largest bourbon collections and its own line of Moonshine – distilled right underneath the restaurant. Also underneath the restaurant is a blues bar making Hendricks more than a place to go for a plate of food.

I found quality across the board with the ribs, pork and pastrami. Hendricks isn't a group of good ole boys who cobbled together a business after making backyard barbecue for years. It's a well thought out, professionally-run operation. It isn't the normal barbecue experience, but I enjoyed it. The ribs are my recommended item of the barbecue favorites, but, if you want to reach outside barbecue, try the burger or pastrami at Hendricks…you won't regret it.

Jack Stack Barbecue

Kansas City, Missouri (4 locations)

www.jackstackbbq.com

Established: 1957

Style: Upscale Kansas City.

Wood: Hickory.

What to try: Something you haven't had before, Beans and Cheesy Corn Bake.

What to avoid: Pretensions about nicer barbecue.

Case Dorman, now President of Jack Stack Barbecue, joined the restaurant in 1978 as "Bean Boy" at the age of 16. With his job of sending out hot beans from the kitchen, Case met his future father-in-law (and a few choice words) when the beans he dispatched were not piping hot.

Jack Stack is now in its third generation of family ownership and Case says the Jack Stack family extends to his employees. With four locations in greater Kansas City, Jack Stack's pitmasters have been with the restaurant for an average of 20 years. The General Managers of each location are equity partners.

Jack Stack is a full-service, upscale dining experience with a love for barbecue. Declaring itself to have the most diverse barbecue in the country, Jack Stack claims to have also created the ubiquitous Cheesy Corn Bake. The menu offers salads, grilled fish, prime rib and steaks, but it's the barbecue that still beckons most patrons.

I recommend trying one of the unique items, but it's hard to go wrong with the burnt ends, beans and Cheesy Corn Bake.

Lillie's Q

Chicago, Illinois (4 locations)
www.lilliesq.com
Established: 2010
Style: Chef-owned, modern, Carolina/Memphis mix.
Wood: Peach.
What to try: Fried chicken, pork, grits, Kool-Aid pickles.
What to avoid: Tri-tip.

The original Lillie's Q is in the trendy Bucktown area just west of downtown Chicago. Named after Owner/Chef Charlie McKenna's grandmother, the restaurant has been well-received by both neighbors and Chicago restaurant critics alike. *Food&Wine Magazine* even named it the "Best new barbeque restaurant in the country" in 2011.

Lillie's Q carries a full line of quality sauces covering the regions of barbecue and it's quite possible they are in a store near you. Chef Charlie describes Lillie's Q as a mix between Carolina and Memphis styles of barbecue, but I would just call it Southern.

The recommended dish for a first time visitor is the Taste of LQ with your choice of three meats. If you want something other than the traditional proteins, try the smoked fried chicken. I love Gus' Fried Chicken in Memphis, but the fried chicken at Lillie's Q may be even better. The stone ground grits with house-made bacon were the best grits I had on the barbecue trail and if you want to try something different, how about Kool-Aid Pickles?

LC's Bar-B-Q

Kansas City, Missouri
Old LC will probably die before they get a website.
Established: 1989
Style: Old-school urban dive.
Wood: Hickory.
What to try: Take your pick.
What to avoid: A barbecue stain on your shirt.

I remember first visiting LC's Bar-B-Q as a teenager. The no frills, smoke-filled, barred-window interior has not changed much since that time. Plans are in the works to open a second restaurant and while the atmosphere of the new place will be different, I'm sure LC will continue to crank out excellent barbecue.

I sat down with the affable LC for a lesson in barbecue. My favorite story stemmed out of a question regarding how he got started in the business. LC replied that as a kid, he cooked hot dogs and hamburgers over a home-made grill. Burning whatever wood he could scavenge, he used a truck rim for the pit with hog wire over the top for the grate.

LC's offers the usual barbecue items, but you should go for the beef or ribs. Add either the regular or hot sauce and enjoy! Just as one might use that last bite of pancake to mop up the syrup, feel free to take your white bread and lap up the last of your sauce.

McGonigle's Market

Kansas City, Missouri

www.mcgonigles.com

Established: 1951

Style: Neighborhood market with a smoker and picnic tables outside.

Wood: Hickory.

What to try: Sausage, burnt ends.

What to avoid: A rainy day.

When McGonigle's opened in 1951, it was located at the point where the pavement of Kansas City turned into a gravel country road. McGonigle's hasn't moved, but is now located in a relatively central part of town. McGonigle's still operates as an independent market with its specialty being unique cuts of meat. In addition to being able to find the likes of beef kidney, one can also purchase McGonigle's refrigerated barbecue for a fresh, yet convenient barbecue option to take home or to Arrowhead Stadium.

McGonigle's began serving barbecue from a trailer years before food trucks were a thing in Kansas City. Business took off, but, despite its loyal following and substantial sales, I had to ask why I never hear it brought up in conversations about Kansas City barbecue restaurants. Some of it probably has to do with it being a take-out place rather than brick and mortar, sit-down restaurant, but some of it probably has to do with it simply being a neighborhood place more than a tourist destination.

The most unique food item from McGonigle's - the barbecue trailer at least - is the Italian sausage roll. Rather than fill a casing with meat, McGonigle's makes their sausage as a pork loin-sized loaf with a few extra binding agents to help hold it together. The lack of casing allows the sausage to easily absorb smoke and creates a different texture. I expect most people to prefer this over the traditional tube sausage.

Despite having eaten a lot of Kansas City barbecue over the years, I had not heard of McGonigle's before it came up in my research for this project. I liked what I found and they earned a spot in the Top 100.

Pappy's Smokehouse

St. Louis, Missouri

www.pappyssmokehouse.com

Established: 2008

Style: Casual, newer-style favorite of St. Louis.

Wood: Apple and cherry.

What to try: Ribs, turkey.

What to avoid: Brisket.

My first restaurant visit on the Barbecue Rankings Tour was with Mike Emerson at Pappy's Smokehouse. As the most recognized barbecue restaurant in St. Louis, Pappy's has gained a national following. Mike Emerson is a 7th generation Missourian and has been around barbecue for a long time.

Shortly after Mike opened Pappy's in 2008, Bobby Flay stopped in. Pappy's website only had 500 visits before Flay's visit, but 5,000 hits within an hour afterwards. Pappy's was then featured on *Man vs. Food* and the lines haven't been short since. The growth, recognition and popularity of Pappy's has been great, and Mike said his biggest challenge is scaling quality.

The ribs are Pappy's signature item. Smoked at 225 for approximately 4.5-5.5 hours, they are tender, meaty and perfectly spiced. Mike said there is nothing in the rub that most people do not have in their pantry- the key is getting the blend just right.

One item you do not see at all smokehouses is smoked turkey, but Pappy's makes the best smoked turkey I found in America. Pappy's started smoking turkey after hearing light-hearted grumblings linking them to the freshmen fifteen at nearby St. Louis University and Harris-Stowe State University. The results beat anything your grandmother made for Thanksgiving. Nothing against grandma, it's the power of smoke.

Q Fanatic

Champlin, Minnesota

www.qfanatic.com

Established: 2007

Style: It's Minnesota, they can do whatever they want and no one knows any better.

Wood: Hickory and apple.

What to try: Slab bacon, burnt ends, Monster Cookie Sundae.

What to avoid: Saying it's too far from Minneapolis. Make the trip.

Q Fanatic in Champlin, Minnesota, is a family-friendly restaurant operated by the friendly Johnson family. Patriarch and Chef, Charlie Johnson, has made his own sauces and smoked ribs since the 80's. Combining his restaurant experience and passion for barbecue, Charlie perfected his menu through catering before opening the brick and mortar Q Fanatic.

With 15 sides and eight sauces accompanying the variety of meat combinations, the menu at Q Fanatic is dizzying. Charlie recommends trying the slab bacon, brisket and pulled ham with sides of beans, potato salad and spicy potato wedges.

I sampled a little bit of everything and was impressed. The smoked slab bacon is absolutely decadent and delicious. The brisket had a perfect flavor profile and the burnt ends were excellent. I appreciate a restaurant with thoughtful sides and the grilled seasonal vegetables, beans and mac 'n cheese were all top-notch additions to the meal. A trip to Q Fanatic is incomplete without the Monster Cookie Sundae. It's a work of art. I made a request, in fact, for a gallery to be created at the Minneapolis Institute of Arts for the Monster Cookie Sundae. I've yet to hear back from them.

Ray Ray's Hog Pit

Columbus, Ohio
www.rayrayshogpit.com
Established: 2009
Style: A little from here, a little from there…
Wood: Pignut hickory and white oak.
What to try: Chicken, brisket.
What to avoid: Desserts.

Many Columbus foodies consider Ray Ray's Hog Pit to put out the best barbecue in town. I don't disagree. The permanently parked food truck shares outdoor seating with the rock club next door, which leads to interesting people watching. Fueled by the University nearby, Ray Ray's has one of the most ardent online followings I have seen and this often translates to a 30-45 minute wait at mealtime.

Ray Ray's is most known for brisket. It's very well done, but certainly isn't the only thing worth trying. I typically prefer spicier or blended sauces with a lot of vinegar, but the sweet sauce was my favorite at Ray Ray's. The ribs were a bit over-rubbed for my taste, but the pulled chicken was terrific and the generous sandwiches came together perfectly.

I love the experience at Ray Ray's. It's a fun, unpretentious place that serves great food.

Salt + Smoke

St. Louis, Missouri
www.saltandsmokestl.com
Established: 2014
Style: Casual-modern, chef background, extensive drinks list.
Wood: Post oak.
What to try: Brisket, Smoked and Fried Jalapeno Cheddar
        Bologna.
What to avoid: Saving Salt + Smoke for last.

On October 21, 2014, I finished the Barbecue Rankings Tour at Salt + Smoke with my 365th restaurant visit. I thought it fitting for my last visit to be a restaurant that opened during my time on the road. Before my visit, I heard good things about Salt + Smoke from friends and read glowing reviews in the press. I was not let down.

As my understanding of barbecue changed throughout the year, I realized I had never had true Texas brisket. Most brisket outside the Lone Star State is basically sliced, cooked beef from the brisket cut. A Texas brisket is a completely different experience. Salt + Smoke isn't exactly like what you will find at some of the celebrated Texas bris+ethouses, but it's the closest thing I found in St. Louis or Kansas City. When you visit, be sure to request the moist part of the brisket. It's fattier, but you only live once.

Another highlight, only to be tried in addition to or after the moist brisket, is the smoked and fried jalapeno cheddar bologna. If bologna isn't your thing (and it isn't mine), think of it as a sausage. It's unique and surprisingly tasty. The ribs were good and I'll take the crusty, light popover to just about any cornbread.

Great food, comfortable atmosphere and intriguing drinks list…what more do you need?

Smokey D's BBQ

Des Moines, Iowa
www.smokeydsbbq.com
Established: 2006
Style: Competition barbecue in a sports bar.
Wood: Cherry.
What to try: Burnt ends, mac 'n cheese.
What to avoid: Iowa in January. It's awful.

The road taken by Darren and Sherry Warth that led to the opening of Smokey D's BBQ is common, but rarely does this road lead to such great success. Darren and Sherry thought they might test the restaurant waters by selling barbecue out of a trailer in their driveway on weekends. When this little project turned into $100,000 of revenue in the first year, they knew they were on to something.

The Warths teamed up with local Chef Shad Kirton and opened a catering space. Almost as soon as they opened, however, they grew out of this space and today have multiple locations around Des Moines including the monstrous 11,000 square feet space that seats over 400 people that I visited.

Smokey D's fields three barbecue competition teams - one lead by Darrin, one by Shad and one for the rest of the staff - and they consider each other their biggest rivals. With recent wins at the *American Royal*, *Kingsford* and *Jack Daniel's* competitions, they are the hottest barbecue competitors in the country.

I sampled the ribs, pork and burnt ends right out of the Ole Hickory Pits smoker and my favorite had to be the tasty burnt ends. While some burnt ends are dry, overly charred, or need sauce, these perfectly balanced the charred goodness of the bark with the tenderness of the interior brisket. For a side, I recommend the mac 'n cheese.

Smoky Jon's #1 BBQ

Madison, Wisconsin

www.smokyjons.com

Established: 1986

Style: College town join doing its own thing and doing it well.

Wood: Green Wisconsin shag hickory.

What to try: Ribs, sausage, mac 'n cheese.

What to avoid: Brisket.

Jon of Smoky Jon's in Madison, Wisconsin, has catered for 40 years and operated his brick and mortar restaurant for 29. He's quite the character and a pioneer in the vast barbecue wilderness that is Wisconsin.

Smoky Jon's is all about the ribs. I preferred the wet over the dry and they were, in fact, pretty darn good. The sauce at Smoky Jon's is also unique. Most barbecue sauces are cooked and blended to such a consistency that thickness is about the only characteristic one notices about texture. Chunky is too strong of a word, but Smoky Jon's sauce has distinct texture.

Jon and I talked shop for a couple hours and I want to share some of our conversation with you. In his own words, here is a little bit more from Jon.

Me: What is your first memory of barbecue?

Jon: My first memory of barbecue came as a young boy smelling the wonderful aroma and billowing smoke that came from charcoal and wood burning pits and grills. I loved the smell of the product cooking and the taste of it even more. My Dad was my first barbecue mentor and my Mom's sides were, and still are, to die for. Barbecue being a family affair made my first memory of barbecue unforgettable.

What can you tell me about barbecue in Madison or Wisconsin as a whole?

Barbecue has grown greatly since I began 40 years ago. When I started, there were hardly any barbecue places in Madison - or in Wisconsin for that matter. Because of the popularity of barbecue and the advent of the Food Channel and other media, barbecue has grown tremendously on a national scale. Wisconsin is no exception to this. There have been four new barbecue places open in Madison this year alone. It's not religion like it is in the South, but good barbecue is going to appeal to a large cross section of the population. Authentic wood-smoked, dry-rubbed, smoky, juicy and tender barbecue served with good side dishes and a great barbecue sauce is what wins here, just like most everywhere.

What makes Smoky Jon's barbecue unique or different?

We pledge allegiance to the "real" barbecue place. Our authentic, wood-cooked barbecue that is smoky, sticky, spicy, saucy, juicy, tender and delicious is our foundation. Our authentic Wisconsin Northwoods Log Cabin décor, complete with wood ceiling, brick floor, shack doors and blues music definitely lets people know where they are and why they are here. Our log walls in our dining room are covered with our awards and accolades we have received. A loaded trophy case displays many of the National Awards we have won for our barbecue. Our dining room tables are covered with red and white gingham checked table covers with roll towels on a wrought iron rack all sitting on a glass table top. Our genuinely friendly and caring employees really care about your experience. We strive for perfection every day. We're not barbecue style, WE ARE BBQ.

If someone gets to stop in at Smoky Jon's one time, what do you recommend they order?

The ribs!

Vernon's BBQ

St. Louis, Missouri
www.vernonsbbq.com
Established: 2012
Style: Memphis with a little bit from here and there.
Wood: Local apple, peach, cherry, mulberry and pear.
What to try: Wings, turkey, cornbread, smoked fruit.
What to avoid: Brisket.

Having grown up with barbecue, extensively traveled the barbecue world and worked with some of St. Louis' favorite barbecue kings, Vernon's owner Matt Stiffelman knows a lot about the craft.

When asked what he considers Vernon's signature dishes, Matt stuck with the brisket, ribs and chicken wings. The brisket wasn't my favorite, but the ribs were good. The wings were awesome. The wings also come with a great story. Matt served his wings at an outdoor concert by the St. Louis Arch when B.B. King, of all people, announced to the crowd that if they wanted to have the best chicken wings of their lives, they needed to go visit Matt. That's quite the endorsement!

I also thought the turkey was quite good. My favorite of the sides were the Smoked Seasonal Fruit (apples during my visit), Matt's Secret Corn Bread, and Tequila Lime Green Beans.

Vernon's is home to one of the more unusual of the 2,000+ sauces I tried along the barbecue trail. Matt didn't invent the Thai peanut sauce, but he brought his spin to barbecue.

I liked Vernon's. It's a comfortable, friendly, neighborhood place where I could go regularly for lunch.

Woody's Smoke Shack

Des Moines, Iowa
www.woodyssmokeshack.com
Established: 2008
Style: Family-friendly, slightly quirky neighborhood spot.
Wood: Cherry.
What to try: Ribs, cheesy jalapeno grits.
What to avoid: Lean brisket.

After years of competitions and catering, Woody and Cheryl Wasson now operate a little place just south of Drake University in Des Moines, Iowa, called Woody's Smoke Shack. The interior seating is quite limited, but the large outdoor space accommodates live music and has enough space for kids to kick around a soccer ball. When the weather is nice, the yard turns into a gathering place where people come to enjoy the evening.

Iowa is America's largest producer of pork with nearly 1/3 of all American hogs calling the Hawkeye state home. The brisket, however, is Woody's biggest seller. Woody said Iowans prefer lean meat, so he only smokes trimmed brisket flats. I'm a fatty brisket guy, though, so it wasn't quite what I look for in a brisket. I was impressed, however, with the scrumptious baby back ribs and the cheesy jalapeno grits. That's a meal I could eat any day. I didn't ask about it at every restaurant, but Woody's was the only barbecue restaurant I found to serve my beloved gooseberry pie. This couldn't, however, make too great of an impression on me since we were outside the limited gooseberry season. I might have to make a trip to Iowa, though, just for Woody's ribs, grits and gooseberry pie.

Texas

I always thought Texans a bit obnoxious when boasting about the greatness of their state. As the great Dizzy Dean liked to say, though, "It ain't braggin' if ya can back it up." When it comes to barbecue, they back it up. I'm a convert.

The Blue Ox BBQ

Austin, Texas

www.bbqfoodtruckaustin.com

Established: 2013

Style: Lumberjack themed food truck adjoined to a coffee shop
serving central Texas 'cue.

Wood: Post oak.

What to try: Pork loin, brisket.

What to avoid: A rainy day.

The Blue Ox is another member of the new barbecue wave in Austin. Owner Chase Palmer quit a corporate job to pursue his passion of barbecue and, in 2013, he opened his own place – The Blue Ox. He has experience working for John Mueller and bought a pit from Aaron Franklin intertwining himself into the fabric of Austin barbecue.

The Blue Ox sits behind Buzz Mill Coffee and the two share a covered, outdoor seating area featuring hand-made furniture.

For the first time visitor, Chase recommends the brisket and beef rib with sides of green beans and German potato salad – both of which feature house-cured bacon. The coffee-rubbed pork loin also jumps off the menu as something unique and different.

The fatty portion of brisket fell apart just as it should. I enjoyed the savory rub on the pulled pork and the ribs were good. It was coffee-rubbed pork loin, however, that won the race by a nose. Pork loin is one of my favorite meats and rarely seen at barbecue restaurants. Moist and smoky without the coffee overpowering the pork, it was sublime.

Freedmen's Bar

Austin, Texas
www.freedmensbar.com
Established: 2012
Style: Tasteful bar meets patio barbecue joint.
Wood: Post oak.
What to try: Pulled pork, brisket, ribs, a cocktail.
What to avoid: Skip the potato salad and sausage. They aren't
        bad, but everything else is better.

The historic building Freedmen's Bar calls home was originally built in 1869 by a freed slave in a settlement called Wheatville. It served as a residence, church, and grocery before becoming a restaurant. Freedmen's Bar retains the building's storied history, even as a modern, trendy and comfortable restaurant and bar.

Executive Chef and Pitmaster Evan LeRoy is carving his place in the up-and-coming generation of Texas pitmasters. Everything at Freedmen's is made in-house including focaccia bread, seven kinds of pickles and a red wine barbecue sauce. Just as barbecue is experiencing a renaissance, especially in Austin, there is also renewed interest in classic cocktails. Freedman's brings the two together.

Chef Evan said a first time guest should try the Texas Trinity plate that includes brisket, pork ribs and sausage with a side of German potatoes and a classic cocktail. The brisket has a wonderfully crunchy bark, the ribs are glazed with house-made jalapeno jelly and the sausage is a classic Texas hot link. The brisket and ribs were quite good, but my favorite item was the pulled pork - not something you expect from a barbecue restaurant in Texas. The apple cider vinegar was front and center and it's some of the best pulled pork you will find anywhere in America.

Hard Eight BBQ

Coppell, Texas (3 locations)
www.hardeightbbq.com
Established: 2003
Style: Open pit.
Wood: Mesquite.
What to try: Ribs, brisket, jalapeno sausage.
What to avoid: Stopping in for just a bite. Come hungry.

I visited Hard Eight BBQ in Coppell, Texas, on the recommendation of a friend who considers it the best in the Dallas-Fort Worth area. Opinions, however, are split. Some who love the original location in Stephenville may consider the Coppell installment too big, too new or too touristy (it's a short hop from the airport). Others don't care for Hard Eight because they do not prefer the open-pit style of barbecue.

I get all of that, but if I could visit 100 of my 365 stops again, Hard Eight makes the list. It wasn't the most historic or unique atmosphere, but it was comfortable. It's a well-run, clean, friendly place and I enjoyed being met with smoke in the parking lot. At the clip of 2.5 cords of mesquite a day, they are producing plenty of smoke. None of the food made a Top 10 list at the end of the book, but I don't have any complaints about my meal. I liked that the 50/50 beef/pork jalapeno sausage had some serious heat. The brisket had good flavor and the ribs were all-around good ribs.

Nothing may exemplify my position on Hard Eight more than the banana pudding. Some restaurants boast about making their banana pudding from scratch, but most use mixes for the pudding. Hard Eight uses pudding mix, but they crumbled the vanilla wafers on top. It's a very minor, easy thing to do, but, after eating dozens of banana puddings around the country, this small touch made the experience a tiny bit better than most.

With so many great barbecue options on my journey, no restaurant could make this list without being great. Rather than a single great item at Hard Eight, though, it was the consistency of quality across the board that made this a great stop.

Hutchins BBQ

McKinney, Texas
www.hutchinsbbq.net
Established: 1978
Style: Family-friendly joint in Suburban Dallas.
Wood: Pecan.
What to try: Brisket, more brisket and pulled pork.
What to avoid: Forgetting the beer, it's BYOB.

Roy Hutchins began selling barbecue in McKinney, Texas, in 1978. Near the entrance, one can find a picture of his son, Tim, crawling in the ash-covered pits. Tim runs the restaurant today with General Manager Dustin Blackwell and I sat down with them to hear the history of Hutchins BBQ, learn about their food and sample their signature items.

Texas is all about brisket and Hutchins does it well. Incredibly well. I was also surprised and impressed with the pulled pork. Rather than the traditional paprika-heavy pork rub, Hutchins uses a black pepper-heavy rub more similar to a traditional brisket rub. The result is some of the best pork I've had anywhere. For dessert, they offer a free dessert bar that includes peach cobbler, banana pudding, soft-serve ice cream and coffee.

Opie's Barbecue

Spicewood, Texas
www.opiesbarbecue.com
Established: 1999
Style: Family-friendly, open pits.
Wood: Mesquite.
What to try: Spicy Ribs, jalapeno cheddar sausage.
What to avoid: Opie's is one of the few places in Texas I
    recommend two meats ahead of the brisket. Just get a bite.

Located west of Austin in the Hill Country, Opie's Barbecue is far enough from Austin to feel like rural Texas, but close enough to still be accessible on a Saturday afternoon.

Opie's has received all sorts of national recognition and press. It feels like classic Texas barbecue with the customer picking meat right off of the warming pit, but it's much more modern, bright and comfortable than most restaurants.

Owners Todd and Kristen recommended the baby back ribs and brisket, but let me try a little bit of everything. The spicy ribs were my favorite, but the jalapeno cheddar sausage was a close second. The spicy corn proved an excellent compliment and I do not expect anyone to be disappointed with the selection of desserts.

Pecan Lodge

Dallas, Texas

www.pecanlodge.com

Established: 2010

Style: Urban setting, old-school flavor.

Wood: Mesquite.

What to try: Brisket.

What to avoid: Sausage.

Of the major barbecue centers (Texas, Kansas City, Memphis and the Carolinas), two of the four are metropolitan areas. Drive an hour from Kansas City to St. Joseph, Missouri, and the barbecue scene is bleak. Drive two hours from Memphis to Little Rock and you'll see the difference. In Texas and the Carolinas, however, the best barbecue is traditionally found in small towns. Llano, Lockhart and Lexington were barbecue destinations from Dallas, Houston and San Antonio. In North Carolina, barbecue from Goldsboro, Smithfield and Lexington has always outshone Charlotte, Raleigh and Winston-Salem.

Just as America has increasingly become a more urban society, barbecue is becoming more urban. Most of the restaurants that made the Top 100 in places like Dallas, San Antonio, Charlotte and Raleigh are relatively new. Barbecue has been found in and around Dallas for years, but it wasn't considered comparable to the small town, historic restaurants until recently. Pecan Lodge is the standard bearer of this movement for Dallas – and Texas. Austin is growing incredibly fast, but the introduction of elite barbecue to the much bigger area of DFW (and North Texas – further away from Lockhart) is a more significant seismic shake to the Texas barbecue landscape.

I found the sauces to be OK and the sides and sausage above average. The pork ribs were quite good and the atmosphere and experience were nice, but none of this would bring me back to Pecan Lodge. I will return, however, for some of the best brisket in America. The tender, smoky slices of beef perfection are what barbecue dreams are made of. Pecan Lodge is one of *Texas Monthly's* favorites for good reason. The bite of fatty brisket at Pecan Lodge is one of the best bites in Texas.

Pody's BBQ

Pecos, Texas
www.facebook.com/PodysBBQ
Established: 2011
Style: Central Texas moved west.
Wood: Post oak for brisket. Pecan, cherry and peach for ribs.
What to try: Pulled pork, brisket, chili-cheese hominy.
What to avoid: Spicy sauce…if you can't handle the heat.

Pecos is an oil town on the western side of Texas. I hustled out of Dallas early one morning to make the long, flat drive west since Pody's BBQ is only open for lunch.

I was glad I made the trip. Pody's is a family-run place with Israel, his mother, sister, aunt and wife making up the entire Pody's team. Israel said it's really the ladies who run the place and I believe him.

Pody's smokes with pecan, cherry or peach woods for ribs and post oak for brisket. All of this wood has to be transported to Pecos as you and I are taller than the vast majority of foliage in this dry and dusty western corner of Texas.

I had a sampler plate and started, as I always do, with the brisket. Pody's brisket is some of the smokiest you will find anywhere. I enjoyed the chili-cheese hominy, which was a nice break from the usual barbecue sides. The ribs were very good. The pinto beans were not my thing, but only because I'm a baked beans kind of guy. I was warned about the ghost pepper hot sauce and, while I used it sparingly, still ended up gulping down a couple glasses of water afterwards.

My final bites ended up being the best. Everything at Pody's was solid, but the pork was stellar. Like all of Pody's meats, the pork has a definitive blackened bark that gives it an excellent charred flavor. The inside was moist, smoky and perfectly pulled. While I expected the quality of pork to deteriorate as I ventured west, Pody's had the best pork I found in Texas and is right there with the best hog you can find anywhere.

Rooster's Roadhouse

Denton, Texas
www.roosters-roadhouse.com
Established: 2008
Style: Roadhouse with food as eclectic as the decorations.
Wood: Hickory.
What to try: Brisket burger, pulled pork nachos.
What to avoid: Comparing it to an Austin joint. Just enjoy
Rooster's Roadhouse for what it is.

This one may be a surprise to a lot of Texans – not because those who visit Rooster's Roadhouse don't care for it, but because it isn't often discussed in barbecue circles. I think Rooster's Roadhouse is passed over because they do things a bit differently. The menu is more roadhouse than brickethouse, but plenty of barbecue items are to be found.

A good barbecue meal often starts, especially in Texas, with a cold beer. Rooster's kegs are housed in a walk-in freezer and the tapped beer runs through 100 feet of stainless steel pipe packed in ice before being served at a nearly frozen 29 degrees. It's basically impossible to get a colder beer in liquid form.

After getting an ice cold beer, sit down and take in the classic barbecue and roadhouse atmosphere that includes neon signs, local paraphernalia, unique pieces and sing-along music.

Open the menu and you will find standard barbecue staples as well as unique barbecue creations. I recommend either the Red Neck Sushi or Pulled Pork Nachos as an appetizer. The Red Neck Sushi consists of brisket, sauce, cheese and chilis wrapped in a flour tortilla and sliced like a sushi roll. The side of pickled onion mimics the pickled ginger served with sushi.

Topped with a generous portion of pork, jalapenos, queso, shredded cheese, pico, beans and barbecue sauce, the Pulled Pork Nachos were also terrific. If you attack these appetizers alone, you will not be disappointed, but you will not make it to the main dishes as they are certainly not kickshaws. Everything at Rooster's is a little bit different, but it's all really darn good. I loved both the brisket burger and pulled pork sandwich on Texas Toast. It's not a true representation of Texas barbecue, but I thought the food was great and it's a fun place. I'll be back.

Smitty's Market

Lockhart, Texas

www.smittysmarket.com

Established: 1999...but they've been doing barbecue in the
building for a long time.

Style: Lockhart. Beautiful, wonderful Lockhart.

Wood: Post oak.

What to try: Sausage, brisket.

What to avoid: Filling up, because you have more places to visit
on a day in Lockhart.

Some readers will care for a restaurant much more than me, while
others not like it nearly as much. If you take my advice to visit
Smitty's in Lockhart, though, I'm fairly confident you will see it as
I see it.

The experience of Smitty's is one-of-a-kind. It can't be beat. From
the dark, smoke-filled pit room to the counter running the length
of a long, picturesque hallway, this is what a barbecue experience
is meant to be.

The barbecue might not be your absolute favorite, but it's good. It may not even be your favorite in Lockhart. This doesn't matter. It still deserves a visit. Brisket and sausage are the obligatory items although other offerings like ribs and clod are available. I preferred the sausage over the brisket.

This is an obligatory stop for any barbecue fan.

SMOKE

Dallas, Texas (2 locations)

www.smokerestaurant.com

Established: 2009

Style: Modern Texan cuisine.

Wood: Oak, hickory, maple.

What to try: A smoked meat creation unlike anything you have tried before.

What to avoid: Expectations. Go with an open mind.

Tim Byres is a decorated chef who used his talents, among other places, at the US Embassy in Brussels before opening SMOKE in Dallas.

Some traditional barbecue folks will consider SMOKE fine dining rather than barbecue - as if it cannot be both. Sure, there is a robust wine menu, cocktail menu that includes a few liquors difficult for old barbecue hands to pronounce, seafood, cloth napkins and modern art, but that doesn't change the fact that the meat of the menu is still…well…smoked meat.

SMOKE has received numerous awards since it opened in 2009. Open for three meals a day, there is often a two hour wait on Sunday mornings for brunch. My meal started with a tasting of the house-cured bacon, andouille sausage, pulled pork and beef rib.

After sampling some of the meats, we moved on to SMOKE's wheelhouse - utilizing smoked meats in refined, interesting dishes. I hadn't had a Pit-Roasted Cabrito and Fresh Masa with goat's milk cajeta and green apple salsa verde anywhere else on the Barbecue Rankings Tour, but I enjoyed it at SMOKE.

If you are in Dallas and looking for authentic, traditional Texas barbecue, this isn't your place. If, however, you would like to expand your barbecue horizons and enjoy a nicer dining experience, SMOKE is the place to go.

Smoke Shack

San Antonio, Texas (2 locations)
www.smokeshacksa.com
Established: 2010
Style: Southern with a Texas twang.
Wood: Pecan and oak.
What to try: Big Dog sandwich.
What to avoid: Expecting traditional Texas barbecue.

Smoke Shack is one of the hot names on the San Antonio barbecue scene. Owner Chris Conger built two portable Smoke Shacks with his own hands and recently opened the first Smoke Shack brick and mortar.

Smoke Shack's top sellers are the coffee-rubbed brisket, pork ribs, and brisket 'n sausage mac 'n cheese. As I do once in a while, I'll actually recommend something other than the best-selling items. You can try the brisket or pulled pork, but try it on a sandwich. Smoke Shack's fresh baked bread makes all the difference. On the side, I recommend the green onion slaw with feta cheese.

Tejas Steakhouse & Saloon

Bulverde, Texas

www.tejasrodeo.com

Established: 2011

Style: A rodeo complex with bars, shops, a rodeo ring and steakhouse.

Wood: Mostly mesquite from the ranch for beef, hickory for pork and occasionally cherry, alder, apple and pecan for other items.

What to try: KC style steak, creamed corn, beans.

What to avoid: Traditional barbecue meats were fine, but certainly not the stars of the show.

The sprawling Tejas Rodeo complex in Bulverde, Texas, is home to professional rodeo events, seven bars, shops, live music and multiple places to find a plate of food. On the Saturday in January of my visit, they expected 1,500 people that evening for the rodeo at the family-owned property that dates back to the 1800's.

Chef Tyler Horstmann oversees all of the food operations. With a background in French/Mediterranean upscale seafood, Tyler is another chef transforming Texas barbecue. A native of San Antonio, there is something comfortable, familial and rewarding about returning to the flavors of his home.

I visited Tejas for the barbecue, but the Tejas Steakhouse & Saloon had recently been given the Editor's Choice Award by *San Antonio Magazine* as the best steakhouse in the area. The barbecue shack is across a courtyard from the steakhouse with outdoor seating near the arena. Both restaurants serve Texas Akaushi beef which descends from the most celebrated lines of Japanese cattle. The quality of the beef may be unmatched at any barbecue restaurant in America. The barbecue highlights were the pulled pork and barbecue sauce. These were accompanied by the best creamed corn anywhere in America and perfect green beans. Tejas makes their own buttermilk used in the creamed corn and the creaminess and sour cream flavor was terrific. The beans, with local bacon and a hint of citrus, were also superb.

I enjoyed my sampling of all of these fares, until Chef Tyler brought me something else to try. The signature dish at the Steakhouse is the KC Cut Tenderloin. It's cooked in a skillet over an open fire and the quality of the beef with the simple salt, pepper, garlic, butter combination made this one of the best things I ate all year. Tejas comes with my highest recommendation, but, just this once, skip the traditional barbecue items and try the KC Tenderloin with the creamed corn and green beans.

The Brisket House

Houston, Texas (2 locations)
www.thebriskethouse.com
Established: 2010
Style: Suburban strip-mall, but the brisket is worth it.
Wood: Oak and pecan.
What to try: Brisket.
What to avoid: The raw, quartered onion. Why Texas, why?

My favorite barbecue restaurant in Houston is The Brisket House. Owner Wayne Kammerl's College Station barbecue roots are on display here. Wayne ran the now closed, but old College Station favorite, Tom's BBQ for seven years. He moved to corporate restaurants, but always knew that when he opened his own place, he wanted it to be barbecue.

As he set up shop in an affluent section of West Houston, Wayne added The Brisket House Special to the menu. On the very first day of operation, an A&M alum noticed that it was basically the Aggie Special from Tom's. With meat options of 6 oz, 8 oz or 1 pound, your choice of brisket, sausage, pork ribs, pulled pork, chicken or turkey comes with a whole pickle, slab of cheddar cheese, quartered white onion and bread.

I was impressed with everything I had at The Brisket House, but you have to try, you guessed it, the brisket. It was one of my favorites in Texas which means it's one of the best anywhere.

Two Bros. BBQ Market

San Antonio, Texas
www.twobrosbbqmarket.com
Established: 2008
Style: Family-friendly neighborhood spot.
Wood: Oak.
What to try: Shiner sauce with brisket, beans.
What to avoid: Running out of sauce.

Two Bros. BBQ Market is a big part of the barbecue revival in San Antonio. Owners Jason and Jake Dady have opened a variety of restaurants around town and Two Bros. has received plenty of attention and praise. The atmosphere at Two Bros. includes a large outdoor space with picnic tables, bocce courts and a playground - all surrounded by a cloud of smoke.

Two Bros.' pitmaster is Emilio Soliz. After moving to Two Bros. from another Dady restaurant, he threw himself fully into the art of smoking meats. The two most popular dishes are the brisket and cherry-glazed baby back ribs. I gave the popular, thick mac 'n cheese the ole Dairy Queen Blizzard test by turning it upside down and it didn't budge. The pinto beans dominant in Texas never became my favorite, but the peaches added to Two Bros.'s pinto beans were a pleasant surprise.

My food recommendation for Two Bros. is a bit more nuanced than normal. The brisket by itself is better than most, but I would not put it in the top tier of Texas briskets. When you add the dark, rich, deep coffee and molasses-like Shiner sauce, though, it's right there with the best brisket around – odd since I wouldn't dare put sauce on any of the others. Old-school barbecue folks in Texas who consider saucing brisket a sin may not want anything to do with this. The sauce is not simply a good barbecue sauce, but it creates its own category separate from nearly all other sauces. Some might compare it to the much publicized espresso barbecue sauce at Franklin in Austin, but Two Bros. is darker, richer, bolder and, to me, better.

Valentina's Tex Mex BBQ

Austin, Texas
www.valentinastexmexbbq.com
Established: 2013

Style: Old family Mexican recipes meet 21st century barbecue.

Wood: Mesquite.

What to try: Tacos.

What to avoid: Indecision. Go with the tacos.

Valentina's TEX MEX BBQ is named after owner Miguel Vidal's beautiful daughter, Valentina. The menu is the blend of Tex-Mex and barbecue Miguel grew up eating. As a 5th-generation Texan from the San Antonio area, his father and uncles manned the smoker at family gatherings while his mother and aunts prepared tortillas, rice and beans in the kitchen. Plates like smoked brisket fajitas were nothing unusual for Miguel - it was just dinner.

After working his way up the restaurant food chain and perfecting his smoking techniques, Miguel pursued his dream to open his own place featuring his family favorites. Each meat is offered as both traditional barbecue and Tex-Mex. The brisket, for example, is used on the Sliced Brisket Sandwich as well as the Smoked Brisket Taco, which comes topped with sea-salt lime guacamole and tomato-serrano salsa. Whichever you choose (and I loved the taco), you will not be disappointed by the charred, smoky, fall-apart-in-your-fingers brisket.

Filled with bars, 6th Street is Austin's most iconic...or notorious...street. I guess it depends on who you ask. Surprisingly, no barbecue restaurants are to be found right on 6th, but Valentina's is only a half block away. Before, during or after a night on 6th, there is no better place to go for a bite.

The Northeast

Nine times out of ten, you are better off sticking with the crab cakes, lobster rolls, cheesesteaks, pizza or clam chowder, but there are a few Northeastern barbecue diamonds in the rough worthy of a visit.

Blackstrap BBQ

Winthrop, Massachusetts
www.blackstrapbbq.com
Established: 2010
Style: Boston can do whatever it wants.
Wood: Mix of fruitwoods.
What to try: Wings, pulled pork with mustard sauce.
What to avoid: Chili-mac. Life is too short to eat chili-mac.

Anchoring the corner of a recently revitalized town square, Blackstrap BBQ serves excellent 'cue to the residents of Winthrop, Massachusetts. During most of my restaurant visits, I found a few items I enjoyed while other items missed the mark. Blackstrap was consistently good across the board.

The wings are a great way to start your meal at Blackstrap and I highly recommend the cumin-heavy buffalo wings. The ribs, pulled pork sandwich and burnt ends sandwich are all equally good. Like other chef-run restaurants in this book, Blackstrap gives plenty of love to their sides which makes for a great all-around meal. The sweet potato salad is a chunky, chilled potato salad with peppers and a lighter mayonnaise sauce. Plain noodles with bean-heavy chili haunt my dreams, but Blackstrap's mac 'n cheese topped with a beanless, meaty, stew-like chili helped me exorcise these demons...but I still believe chili-mac to be a crime against humanity. Go for the pulled pork.

If the mustard sauce isn't on the table, be sure to ask for it. It's fantastic.

garden district

Washington, D.C.
www.gardendistrictdc.com
Established: 2011
Style: D.C. beer garden with an original barbecue style.
Wood: Pecan, apple and mesquite.
What to try: Beer and a brisket sandwich.
What to avoid: December – February. Closed for winter.

One of the men behind garden district, Tad Curtz, is a well-traveled barbecue connoisseur. I enjoyed digging into the recesses of my barbecue-drenched brain to reminisce about the old-school places in North Carolina, Memphis and Texas we both love.

To his credit, he is underspoken about the barbecue at garden district. Tad is also part of one of D.C.'s best pizza joints (2 Amy's – try the Etna). He understands how to make good food and a comfortable dining experience. Tad says he can't compete with the generations-old places in the south, but "works hard to squeak out something better than average."

garden district has done more than beat the average. Brisket is the recommended meat, but, by itself, garden district's brisket isn't quite there with the best of Texas. It did, however, make for a great sandwich. Despite not being very hungry from having eaten barbecue a couple hours earlier, I just kept eating this sandwich.

Ultimately, garden district made the Top 100 because this is a place I want to visit again and again. Yes, the beer and the patio is a big part of it, but I also look forward to having another brisket sandwich.

Hill Country Barbecue Market

Washington, D.C. (2 locations in NYC)
www.hillcountryny.com
Established: NY - 2007, DC - 2011
Style: Texas, but still comfortable to the cosmopolitan
      Northeasterner.
Wood: Aged post oak shipped from Texas.
What to try: Fatty brisket and hot link.
What to avoid: Haters. Let 'em hate.

It seems popular to be a Hill Country hater. Anytime a restaurant receives as much attention as the New York and D.C. installments have received, there will be detractors. First, some Texans say that anything served in New York or D.C. could never live up to Texas standards. Other Texans, by the way, love it. Second, you have a faction of barbecue people who, for one reason or another, turn their nose up at it. Some simply prefer other styles of barbecue. Another group thinks Hill Country is good, but not worth all of the attention and praise it receives. A few, I think, simply want to view themselves as more in-tune with the restaurant scene and, thus, prefer a newer, smaller or less-recognized place. One local told me it's good, but overpriced. Everyone has an opinion.

I don't care. I liked it. Perhaps it was because my bites of fatty brisket were the first bites of a quality brisket I had eaten after months exploring the East Coast, but those bites took me right back to Texas. Yes, it's a big production in a big city. The restaurant can never be exactly like what you might find on a highway in rural Texas, but they go to great lengths to do their best. Most impressively, they ship aged post oak and Kreuz' sausages halfway across the country.

I thought the fatty brisket was great. I also really enjoyed their hot link. Even though Kreuz' sausage is much-beloved in Texas and Hill Country goes to great lengths to ship them to the East Coast, I actually preferred the house-made hot link.

Porky's Place BBQ

York, Pennsylvania (2 locations)

www.porkysplacebbq.com

Established: 1998

Style: Small town, funky little barbecue shack.

Wood: Apple.

What to try: Pork wings.

What to avoid: Don't forget to sign the pig in the front yard.

Porky's Place BBQ is York, Pennsylvania's, spot for barbecue. Joe Oaster, former President of the National Barbecue Association, and his wife run the joint out of an ever changing configuration of buildings. I sampled most of the meats including the ribs and pulled pork, but it was the pork wings that stood out. Years of eating, sleeping and breathing barbecue have led to consistent, quality que at Porky's Place.

After the pork wings, be sure to stop by Maple Donut for something sweet and the Shoe House for a photo and/or tour.

Salvage BBQ

Portland, Maine

www.salvagebbq.com

Established: 2013

Style: Open, artistic, retro loft with Eastern Carolina and Texas
    barbecue.

Wood: Maine red oak.

What to try: Brisket, mac 'n cheese.

What to avoid: Giving up on them. A trusted barbecue writer has
    had mixed experiences at Salvage. Perhaps the consistency
    isn't yet there. If you catch them on a bad day, they are
    worth another look because I nearly put them in the Top 25.

With a number of successful concepts under their belts, a group of
Portland, Maine, restaurateurs set out on a trip across the
Carolinas and Texas to learn from the best in barbecue. Upon
returning with recipes, flavors and techniques, they converted a
historic mail-sorting center into Salvage BBQ. The space, with the
combination of modern and retro elements, and a splash of
junkyard, is welcoming.

I didn't have high expectations for barbecue in Maine, but Salvage
was a very pleasant surprise. Despite Salvage considering Eastern
Carolina to be their greatest region of influence, it was the spicy,
tender brisket that I enjoyed most. The ribs, sausage, mac 'n

cheese and hush puppies were also quite good. Salvage has an interesting line of sauces, some of which change seasonally. I tried a maraschino-habanero that was unlike anything I found elsewhere in the states.

Sweet Lucy's Smokehouse

Philadelphia, Pennsylvania

www.sweetlucys.com

Established: 2003.

Style: Home cooking barbecue conglomeration.

Wood: Hickory.

What to try: Ribs, sweet potatoes, beans.

What to avoid: Brisket.

The GPS was usually my trusted sidekick as I visited new places across the country. Unfortunately, from time to time, the GPS steered me off course and I found myself on a closed road, at an abandoned building or on the wrong street. As I approached Sweet Lucy's, I was confident I was on the wrong trail since I was surrounded by nothing but fenced-in warehouses next to a railroad. When I arrived at 7500 State Road, however, I realized I had given up too easily. I found Sweet Lucy's Smokehouse tucked into the corner of a warehouse.

Sweet Lucy's has received a lot of local press over the last decade and it all started when they were named the best food truck in Philly - a town teeming with food trucks. The food truck evolved into the warehouse restaurant and now barbecue fans from all over the Philadelphia area make the trip to take in the best barbecue in town.

Brook and Jim Higgins have varied culinary backgrounds. The two met in a kitchen and have been cooking together ever since. Jim attributed much of Sweet Lucy's success to a "fussing over everything" attitude as he and Brook run a tight ship.

I found the pork, chicken, wings to all be good, but the ribs stood above the rest. There is nothing particularly different about them, but with great flavor, char, consistency and spice, they were excellent. Sweet Lucy's also puts a lot of effort into their sides and the sweet potatoes and beans were both great.

The West

"That sure puts the pig meat in the fire!" is an old cowboy saying meaning something good just happened and it's time to celebrate. Pork perfection, however, is achieved by keeping the pig out of the fire and in the smoke. Most of the West has yet to figure this out. I found six restaurants, however, that are doing things the right way.

The Boar's Nest

Seattle, Washington
www.ballardbbq.com
Established: 2011
Style: Tennessee-ish…
Wood: Hickory.
What to try: Fried mac 'n cheese, pulled pork.
What to avoid: Ribs - if you don't like them falling off the bone.

Owner Gabe Gagliardi has a classic barbecue story. A native of Tennessee, it took a few years at a desk job for him to figure out that food was his passion. After culinary school in Chicago and working at a number of fine dining establishments around the country, he returned to his barbecue roots and opened The Boar's Nest.

Competition barbecue aficionados prefer ribs to have a little tug to them, but the general public prefers fall-off-the-bone ribs. I'm somewhere in between. As I picked up the ribs at The Boar's Nest, they literally fell off the bone. The pork was smoky, but in no way oversmoked. The delicious fried mac 'n cheese balls were creamy and perfect while the panko coating on the fried pickles added welcome crunch to a fried item that often seems soggy and flimsy.

I found The Boar's Nest to be a nice all-around barbecue spot. It was my favorite of my visits to the Pacific Northwest and the fried mac 'n cheese balls alone are worth the trip.

Bravo Farms Smokehouse

Visalia, California
www.bravofarmsvisalia.com
Established: 2012
Style: Slightly-upscale California blend.
Wood: Mostly oak and cherry.
What to try: Pulled pork, slaw, mixed salad.
What to avoid: Ribs, tri-tip, chicken.

Bravo Farms Smokehouse caught my eye since it is a modern place that combines classic barbecue dishes with steakhouse favorites. Its style reminded me of Chicago q, the nicest barbecue restaurant out of my 365 visits. Interestingly enough, I learned that Chicago q is one of the restaurants Bravo Farms Smokehouse drew inspiration from for the food, feel and experience.

While dinner is full service, lunch consists of a sandwich, wrap and salad line. I was all too happy to sample the tri-tip on a bed of greens. The salad options at Bravo Farms were great, but, in all my time in California, I never developed an appreciation for tri-tip.

The slightly sweet, moist pulled pork was very well done. The accompanying slaw tasted like the cabbage had been picked that morning.

Gorilla Barbeque

Pacifica, California

www.gorillabbq.com

Established: 2006

Style: A shack with an attitude and a little surfer spirit.

Wood: Almond. Save water – burn the almond trees!

What to try: Mac 'n cheese, pulled pork with sauce.

What to avoid: Brisket.

Gorilla Barbeque is situated on scenic Highway 1, a stone's throw from the Pacific Ocean and just a short drive from San Francisco. It's a take-out place built into a 55' railroad car. Gorilla makes for the kind of place that does well on TV and you have likely seen it on the *Food Network*. It's often a scheduled stop for people making the Highway 1 trip up or down the coast, but be prepared to wait. The line typically starts at 11AM for their noon opening. The crew works efficiently, though, to keep things moving.

The mac 'n cheese is some of the best mac 'n cheese I've ever had. As I write this, I'm checking ticket prices to San Francisco just because I want more of this mac 'n cheese…right now. The ribs were good, but the pulled pork was my favorite meat because Gorilla has an excellent peppery, tomato-based sauce of which I could not get enough.

Memphis Minnie's Barbeque Joint & Smokehouse

San Francisco, California

www.memphisminnies.com

Established: 2000

Style: 1% Memphis/99% Haight.

Wood: White Oak and hickory.

What to try: Brisket, greens, mac 'n cheese.

What to avoid: Beef ribs, pork ribs.

Memphis Minnie's is the oldest barbecue spot in San Francisco and sometimes the oldies are still the goodies. The walls are adorned with shirts and knick-knacks from recognized barbecue restaurants across the country in this tight, eclectic and friendly barbecue joint.

Don't visit Memphis Minnie's expecting Memphis-style barbecue. It has its own style. Everything is served dry. My favorite meat was the brisket – a word only spoken in a hushed voice in Memphis. It wasn't an aberration, either, as I was told Memphis Minnie's is equally proud of their brisket and pulled pork. I admit that eating tri-tip for days on end made the brisket probably taste a little better, but I was impressed.

Equally as impressive were the greens. Before trying them, I was told that the greens, along with most of the sides, are vegetarian.

Most barbecue restaurants proudly boast that their greens have bacon, pork, grease or some sort of other sort of non-veggie yummies, but that's not how it's done in San Francisco. I actually loved them. For me it's about having a non-soggy green with the right amount of vinegar and citrus. Memphis Minnie's greens were just that. The mac 'n cheese was also a stand-out side. There were a couple items I wasn't as excited about, but a plate of brisket, greens and mac 'n cheese from Memphis Minnie's will make me happy any day.

R&R Barbeque

Salt Lake City, Utah
www.randrbbq.net
Established: 2013
Style: Blended.
Wood: Oak.
What to try: Brisket, okra.
What to avoid: Pork.

There is no stereotypical barbecue owner. Everyone has their own story, but winning the 1974 US Surfing Championship has to be one of the more unique backgrounds I uncovered.

Brothers Roger and Rodney's venture into barbecue is quickly becoming one of Salt Lake City's favorite spots. I found a lot of average barbecue in Salt Lake City, but R&R was the only one that really stood above the fray. R&R is proud of their brisket – and for good reason. It was the best I found west of Texas. The item that really stood out to me, however, was the okra. It was light, perfectly cooked and the best okra I found in America.

Russell's Smokehouse

Denver, Colorado
www.russellssmokehouse.com
Established: 2011
Style: Date night meets barbecue.
Wood: Mesquite, hickory and apple.
What to try: Loaded Chips, half-chicken, mustard sauce.
What to avoid: Brisket, ribs.

My visit to Russell's Smokehouse in Denver was a story of highs and lows. Opened by Chef/Restauranteur Frank Bonanno, a high level of professionalism was brought to the concept, but the main barbecue dishes were somewhat disappointing. I can't recommend the brisket or ribs. The pulled pork was redeemed by a terrific, vinegar-heavy mustard sauce.

On the other hand, my two best bites anywhere in Colorado (Loaded Chips and half-chicken) came from Russell's. Considering the state of barbecue in Colorado, this wouldn't be enough to get them in the Top 100, but those two dishes were two of the best dishes, of their kind, I found anywhere. The Loaded Chips were even a notch better than Central's BBQ Nachos and the half-chicken placed in my Top 10 Chicken dishes.

Perhaps I hit them on an off day with the standard barbecue items. Due to the excellence of the chicken, nachos, and mustard sauce, I'm willing to try the main proteins again.

Awards

After eating plentiful pounds of pork and bountiful heaps of beef, it took something special to rise above the quagmire of average, or even good, barbecue to be truly great. Most of the names below are for restaurants that made the Top 100. There are a few restaurants, however, who had an amazing dish, but did not do enough with the rest of the meal to make the Top 100.

10 Best Restaurants for Pulled/Chopped Pork in America

1. Payne's Bar-B-Q – Memphis, Tennessee
2. Skylight Inn – Ayden, North Carolina
3. Lexington Barbecue – Lexington, North Carolina
4. Pody's BBQ – Pecos, Texas
5. Hutchins BBQ – McKinney, Texas
6. Freedmen's Bar – Austin, Texas
7. Allen & Son Bar-B-Q – Chapel Hill, North Carolina
8. Smokin Pig: The BBQ Joint – Pooler, Georgia
9. Heirloom Market BBQ – Atlanta, Georgia
10. The Pit Authentic Barbecue – Raleigh, North Carolina

America's 10 Best Pork Ribs

1. Hometown Bar-B-Que – Brooklyn, New York
2. Kerlin BBQ – Austin, Texas
3. Bogart's Smokehouse – St. Louis, Missouri
4. Joe's Kansas City – Kansas City, Kansas
5. Herman's Ribhouse – Fayetteville, Arkansas
6. Dreamland Bar-B-Que – Tuscaloosa, Alabama
7. Double J Smokehouse & Saloon – Memphis, Tennessee
8. Central BBQ – Memphis, Tennessee
9. B.B. King's Blues Club – Memphis, Tennessee
10. Puckett's Grocery and Restaurant – Franklin, Tennessee

5 Best Briskets in Texas

1. Kerlin BBQ – Austin, Texas
2. Franklin BBQ – Austin, Texas
3. Pecan Lodge – Dallas, Texas
4. Hutchins BBQ – McKinney, Texas
5. The Brisket House – Houston, Texas

10 Best Briskets outside Texas (better than 99% in Texas)

1. Hometown Bar-B-Que – Brooklyn, New York
2. 4 Rivers Smokehouse – Winter Garden, Florida
3. Full Service BBQ – Maryville, Tennessee
4. City Butcher and Barbecue – Springfield, Missouri
5. J.R.'s Rhodehouse BBQ Pit – Piedmont, South Dakota
6. Midwood Smokehouse – Charlotte, North Carolina
7. Hill Country Barbecue Market – Washington, D.C.
8. R&R BBQ – Salt Lake City, Utah
9. Smoque BBQ – Chicago, Illinois
10. Salvage BBQ – Portland, Maine

10 Best Sausages in America

1. Black's Barbecue – Lockhart, Texas
2. City Butcher and Barbecue – Springfield, Missouri
3. Martin's Bar-B-Que Joint – Mt. Juliet, Tennessee
4. Opie's Barbecue – Spicewood, Texas
5. Hill Country Barbecue Market (house-made hot link) – Washington, D.C.
6. McGonigle's Market – Kansas City, Missouri
7. Top of the Hill Grill – Brattleboro, Vermont
8. Hard Eight BBQ – Coppell, Texas
9. Smitty's Market – Lockhart, Texas
10. Art's Barbecue (hot link) – Fort Smith, Arkansas

5 Best Burnt Ends in America

1. The Shaved Duck – St. Louis, Missouri
2. Jon Russell's Kansas City Barbeque – Overland Park, Kansas
3. J.R.'s Rhodehouse BBQ Pit – Piedmont, South Dakota
4. City Butcher and Barbecue – Springfield, Missouri
5. Gates Bar-B-Q – Kansas City, Missouri

The Top Chicken in the Land

1. Herman's Ribhouse (smoked breast with garlic sauce) – Fayetteville, Arkansas
2. Lillie's Q (smoked fried chicken) – Chicago, Illinois
3. Momma's Mustard, Pickles & BBQ (smoked wings) – Louisville, Kentucky
4. Blue Smoke (smoked breast) – New York, New York
5. Big Bob Gibson Bar-B-Q (smoked with white sauce) – Decatur, Alabama
6. Mike & Jeff's BBQ (pulled) – Greenville, South Carolina
7. Chicago q (smoked wings) – Chicago, Illinois
8. Blackstrap BBQ (wings) – Winthrop, Massachusetts

9. Russell's Smokehouse (smoked half chicken) – Denver, Colorado

10. Dead End BBQ (George's Competition Chicken – smoked breast) – Knoxville, Tennessee

America's 10 Best Barbecue Sandwiches

Normally, when you have great meat, you don't want to get sauce, bread or anything else to get in the way. The best sandwiches, however, were not necessarily from restaurants with the best meat, but restaurants that added great elements around their good (or great) meat.

1. Payne's Bar-B-Q (Pork sandwich with slaw) – Memphis, Tennessee

2. Smoke Shack BBQ (Big Dog Sandwich) – San Antonio, Texas

3. 17th Street BBQ (Lotta Bull Sandwich) – Murphysboro, Illinois

4. Jon Russell's Kansas City Barbeque (Jon Russell Sandwich) – Overland Park, Kansas

5. Bar-B-Cutie (Pork Sandwich on Cornbread) – Nashville, Tennessee

6. Joe's Kansas City (Z-Man) – Kansas City, Kansas

7. B.T.'s Smokehouse (Brisket Reuben) – Sturbridge, Massachusetts

8. Yellow Dog Eats (Take your pick of the pulled pork sandwiches) – Gotha, Florida

9. garden district (Brisket sandwich) – Washington, D.C.

10. Rocklands Barbeque and Grilling Company (pulled pork with slaw and plenty of sauce) – Arlington, Virginia

The 10 Best Non-Traditional Meats or Main Dishes

1. The Granary Cue and Brew (Beef Clod) - San Antonio, Texas
2. Tejas Steakhouse & Saloon (KC steak) – Bulverde, Texas
3. Cooper's Old Time Pit Bar-B-Que (Big Chop) – Llano, Texas
4. Double J Smokehouse & Saloon (Pork Steak) – Memphis, Tennessee
5. Valentina's TEX MEX BBQ (Brisket Taco) – Austin, Texas
6. Salt + Smoke (Smoked and Fried Bologna) – St. Louis, Missouri
7. Jimmy's BBQ (Smoked Bacon) – Malvern, Pennsylvania
8. Smokin' Okies Catering and Mobile Smokehouse (SOB – Smokin' Okies Burrito) – Oklahoma City, Oklahoma
9. Stubby's Bar-B-Que (Smoked Ham) – Hot Springs, Arkansas
10. Hogshead Café (The Hog Dog) – Richmond, Virginia (Deep fried bacon wrapped jumbo beef hot dog topped with pulled pork, barbecue sauce and slaw)

America's 10 Best Vinegar/Tomato-Based Sauces

1. Skylight Inn (house – strong vinegar, peppery)– Ayden, North Carolina
2. Dreamland Bar-B-Que (original – perfect blend of vinegar and tomato) – Tuscaloosa, Alabama
3. Gates Bar-B-Q (original – tomato-based, black pepper spicy) – Kansas City, Missouri
4. Gorilla Barbeque (house – tomato-based, black pepper spicy with a bit more vinegar) – Pacifica, California
5. Kerlin BBQ (house – the meat is too good to sauce, but take Kerlin's sauce with you) – Austin, Texas
6. SMOKEOUT BBQ (house – blended vinegar and tomato) – Columbus, Ohio

7. Two Bros. BBQ Market (Shiner – dark, rich, made with molasses, coffee and Shiner) – San Antonio, Texas
8. Hicks Bar-B-Que Company (Sweet with a Kick – exactly what the name says) – Belleville, Illinois
9. Maurice's Piggie Park BBQ (Hot Pepper Sauce) – Columbia, South Carolina
10. Boone's Bar-B-Que Kitchen (Eastern Carolina) – Charlotte, North Carolina

America's 5 Best Mustard-based Barbecue Sauces

1. Henry's Smokehouse – Greenville, South Carolina
2. Double J Smokehouse & Saloon – Memphis, Tennessee
3. Blackstrap BBQ – Winthrop, Massachusetts
4. Mike & Jeff's BBQ – Greenville, South Carolina
5. Russell's Smokehouse – Denver, Colorado

Top-Notch Nachos

1. Russell's Smokehouse – Denver, Colorado
2. Central BBQ – Memphis, Tennessee
3. Rooster's Roadhouse – Denton, Texas

Three Turkeys that will put Grandma to Shame

1. Pappy's Smokehouse – St. Louis, Missouri
2. J.R.'s Rhodehouse BBQ Pit – Piedmont, South Dakota
3. Vernon's BBQ – University City, Missouri

The Top Three Beef Ribs I Ate in my Year of Barbecue

1. Hometown Bar-B-Que – Brooklyn, New York
2. Momma's Mustard, Pickles & BBQ – Louisville, Kentucky
3. Dave Poe's BBQ – Marietta, Georgia

5 Best Baked Beans in America

1. Community Q BBQ– Decatur, Georgia
2. Jack Stack Barbecue – Kansas City, Missouri
3. Joe's Kansas City – Kansas City, Kansas
4. Hometown Bar-B-Que – Brooklyn, New York
5. Smoke Daddy – Chicago, Illinois

5 Best Slaws in America

1. Rendezvous (spicy mustard and vinegar) – Memphis, Tennessee
2. Dempsey's BBQ (bacon, cilantro slaw) – Concordia, Missouri
3. Lexington Barbecue (Carolina slaw at its finest) – Lexington, North Carolina
4. Payne's Bar-B-Que (neon yellow and mustardy) – Memphis, Tennessee
5. Kerlin BBQ (bleu cheese slaw) – Austin, Texas

5 Best Potato Sides in America

1. Capitalist Pig (warm potato salad, dressed to order with a vinegar and tarragon sauce) – St. Louis, Missouri
2. Hickory Hollow (deep-fried battered balls of mashed potatoes, cheese, jalapeno, sour cream and bacon) – Houston, Texas
3. One and Only BBQ (twice baked potato salad) – Memphis, Tennessee
4. Holy Smoke BBQ and Grill (bacon ranch potato salad) – Layton, Utah
5. Bone Daddy's House of Smoke (roadhouse cheese spuds) – Dallas, Texas

3 Best Corn Sides

1. Tejas Steakhouse & Saloon (sour cream and homemade buttermilk creamed corn) – Bulverde, Texas
2. Jack Stack Barbecue (cheesy corn bake) – Kansas City, Missouri
3. Smoke Ring (chipotle corn on the cob with cotija cheese) – Atlanta, Georgia

5 Best Grits from the Barbecue Rankings Tour

1. Lillie's Q – Chicago, Illinois
2. Chicago q – Chicago, Illinois
3. Bacon & Caviar – Nashville, Tennessee
4. Eli's Barbeque – Cincinnati, Ohio
5. Woody's Smoke Shack – Des Moines, Iowa

The Three Best Brunswick Stews I found in all the Land

1. Boone's Bar-B-Que Kitchen – Charlotte, North Carolina
2. White Swan BBQ – Smithfield, North Carolina
3. Heirloom Market BBQ – Atlanta, Georgia

Best Mac 'n Cheese in America

1. J.R.'s Rhodehouse BBQ Pit – Piedmont, South Dakota
2. Gorilla Barbeque – Pacifica, California
3. The Boar's Nest (fried mac 'n cheese balls) – Seattle, Washington
4. Chicago q – Chicago, Illinois
5. Salvage BBQ – Portland, Maine

America's Top 3 Greens

1. Sweet Fire Donna's Barbecue and Hops – Alexandria, Virginia
2. Memphis Minnie's – San Francisco, California
3. Heirloom Market BBQ – Atlanta, Georgia

10 Best Other Sides

1. R&R BBQ (fried okra) – Salt Lake City, Utah
2. Smoke Ring (fried green tomato) – Atlanta, Georgia
3. Maurice's Piggie Park BBQ (hash 'n rice) – Columbia, South Carolina
4. Vernon's BBQ (cornbread) – University City, Missouri
5. Tejas Steakhouse & Saloon (green beans) – Bulverde, Texas
6. Salvage BBQ (hushpuppies) – Portland, Maine
7. Skylight Inn (cornbread) – Ayden, North Carolina
8. Henry's Smokehouse (sweet potatoes) – Greenville, South Carolina
9. Lillie's Q (Kool-Aid pickles) – Chicago, Illinois
10. Chicago q (chips) – Chicago, Illinois

5 Best Barbecue Restaurant Desserts in America

1. Enoch's BBQ (Carrot Cake) – Springfield, Missouri*
2. Q Fanatic (Monster Cookie Sundae) – Lake Champlin, Minnesota
3. Sweet Rack Rib Shack (Bourbon Pecan Cheesecake) – Troy, Alabama
4. Branch BBQ (Homemade Ice Cream) – Austin, Texas
5. Smoque BBQ (Pecan Bread Pudding) – Chicago, Illinois

*After the Barbecue Rankings Tour, Enoch's permanently closed. RIP, the best carrot cake I've ever had. Rest in peace…

10 Best Atmospheres in Barbecue

1. Smitty's Market (Smoky pits, everything is old. Lockhart experience that defines Texas barbecue) – Lockhart, Texas
2. Rendezvous (I would pay just to look at the walls. Historic, fun, bustling and the best urban barbecue atmosphere in America) – Memphis, Tennessee
3. Mike & Jeff's BBQ (Perhaps the most hole-in-the-wall of all my visits) – Greenville, South Carolina
4. Dreamland Bar-B-Que (Old-school, dark and a great setting to get messy with some ribs) – Tuscaloosa, Alabama
5. Chicago q (Upscale, clean design) – Chicago, Illinois
6. Kerlin BBQ (Outside, live music, yard games, sometimes free beer) – Austin, Texas
7. Puckett's Grocery and Restaurant (Hear Nashville's soon-to-be stars) – Franklin, Tennessee
8. Franklin Barbecue (The line is worth experiencing…once) – Austin, Texas
9. B.B. King's Blues Club (Great live music and bar) – Memphis, Tennessee
10. garden district (Beer garden and barbecue. Enough said.) – Washington, D.C.

Dream Meals

On the Barbecue Rankings Tour, I often dreamed of combining my favorite elements from restaurants to create a once-in-a-lifetime barbecue meal. Here are five of my dream meals - one for each primary barbecue region and one for the rest of the country. I've picked two main dishes, two sides, a sauce, a drink and a location for each.

Dream Memphis Meal
Main 1: Payne's Pork Sandwich with Slaw
Main 2: Double J's Ribs
Side 1: One and Only's Twice Baked Potato Salad
Side 2: Central's Nachos
Sauce: Double J's Mustard
Drink: Ghost River beer
Setting: Rendezvous

Dream Carolina Meal
Main 1: Skylight Inn Pork
Main 2: Lexington Barbecue Pork
Side 1: Boone's Brunswick Stew
Side 2: Lexington Barbecue Slaw

Sauce: Skylight Inn
Drink: Ashville craft-beer variety pack
Setting: Hilton Head

Dream Kansas City Meal
Main 1: Jon Russell's Burnt Ends
Main 2: Joe's Kansas City Ribs
Side 1: Jack Stack Beans
Side 2: Joe's Kansas City Beans
Sauce: Gates
Drink: Boulevard Wheat
Location: Arrowhead Stadium pre-game

Dream Texas Meal
Main 1: Kerlin Fatty Brisket
Main 2: Cooper's Big Chop
Side 1: Tejas Creamed Corn
Side 2: Hickory Hollow Potatoes
Sauce: Not allowed
Drink: Shiner
Location: Wide-open Texas ranch

Dream Meal from the rest of America
Main 1: Hometown Brisket (Brooklyn, New York)
Main 2: Bogart's Ribs (St. Louis, Missouri)
Side 1: Community Q Baked Beans (Decatur, Georgia)
Side 2: R&R Fried Okra (Salt Lake City, Utah)
Sauce: Dreamland (Tuscaloosa, Alabama)
Drink: Tallgrass Brewing Company Buffalo Sweat Stout
Location: My house with barbecue friends from *The 100 Best Barbecue Restaurants in America*

Thanks for coming along on the journey. I hope you enjoyed the ride, learned something and will use this book as a guide to find America's best barbecue.

Keep on smokin'.

-JDF

Consulting

A tweak in the menu generating 5% growth in sales, a streamlining of processes saving an employee a few minutes each day or a change in smoking techniques that takes your food from good to great is the difference between a surviving restaurant and a thriving business. Johnny has seen the good, the bad and the ugly and he wants to help you make great barbecue, share great barbecue with your community and make some money in the process.

Testimonial from Cara and Dave who opened a barbecue restaurant in Maryland:

Despite our many years in the restaurant business and Dave's accomplished career as a chef, we were so glad to have met with Johnny before opening our barbecue restaurant. He gave us lots of insight into the barbecue scene across the country and gave us a ton of good ideas. His advice and recommendations greatly influenced our menu, and, after a few months of being open, things are going well!

Interested in on-site or virtual consulting? Contact Johnny at barbecuerankings@gmail.com.

Thanks

First, I want to thank the kind, hard-working and generous people from my 365 restaurant visits. I especially want to thank Mike Emerson of Pappy's Smokehouse. I will not forget his encouragement during my very first restaurant visit.

Thanks to Steve Moergen, Mike Armstrong and my dad for their editing assistance.

Thanks are in order to friends and family I stayed with around the country. You kept me going and enriched my road-weary soul.

Thanks to the many people who helped spread the word of this project. From social media faithful like Andrew Eaton and Michael Dawson to those in traditional media, I couldn't have made this a success without you.

Finally, thanks to my family – mom, dad, sis and brother-in-law – who, if they had their doubts about my crazy project, hid them behind words of encouragement.

Top 100 Index

Almost all of the information in this book came from interviews with restaurant owners, managers, pitmasters, staff and barbecue writers. Some of it came from the restaurants' websites. The rest of it came from these resources:

http://blog.estately.com/2014/07/the-mostleast-barbecue-crazed-states-in-america/

http://anthonybourdain.tumblr.com/post/65527686287/parental-advisory-this-program-is-for-mature-adults

http://www.ted.com/talks/malcolm_gladwell_on_spaghetti_sauce?language=en

http://www.slate.com/articles/life/food/2012/08/jell_o_and_mormonism_the_stereotype_s_surprising_origins_.html

http://www.free-times.com/restaurants/a-kinder-gentler-face-for-maurices-piggie-park

http://www.charlestoncitypaper.com/HaireoftheDog/archives/2014/02/24/maurice-bessinger-bbq-baron-and-unrepentant-racist-dies

http://www.al.com/entertainment/index.ssf/2014/09/alabamas_best_bbq_ribs_finalis_8.html

http://www.ncbi.nlm.nih.gov/pubmed?Db=pubmed&Cmd=ShowDetailView&TermToSearch=16891352

http://cowboyspirit.com/cowboy-quotes-10-old-west-sayings-worth-remembering-55/

http://www.goodreads.com/author/quotes/62875.Freya_Stark

The Upside of Irrationality by Dan Ariely. Harper Perennial.

Peace, Love, and Barbecue by Mike Mills and Amy Mills Tunnicliffe. Rodale Press, Inc.

My Life in France by Julia Child. Anchor.

CPSIA information can be obtained
at www.ICGtesting.com
Printed in the USA
FFOW03n0642071115
18448FF